English and Soft Skills

English and Soft Skills

S P Dhanavel

Orient BlackSwan

ENGLISH AND SOFT SKILLS

ORIENT BLACKSWAN PRIVATE LIMITED

Registered Office
3-6-752 Himayatnagar, Hyderabad 500 029, Telangana, INDIA
E-mail: centraloffice@orientblackswan.com

Other Offices
Bengaluru, Bhopal, Chennai, Guwahati, Hyderabad, Jaipur, Kolkata
Lucknow, Mumbai, New Delhi, Noida, Patna, Vijayawada

First published 2010
Reprinted 2010, 2013, 2015, 2016

Cover and book design

ISBN 978 81 250 3980 8

023339
26052016

Typeset in CG Times 11/13.2 *by*
OSDATA, Hyderabad 500 029

Printed in India at
Ashwin Printing Agency, Chennai 600 014

Published by
Orient Blackswan Private Limited
160, Anna Salai, Chennai 600 002
email: chennai@orientblackswan.com

Contents

Publisher's Acknowledgements

Ruskin Bond, 'The Boy Who Broke the Bank'. Copyright © by Ruskin Bond. Reproduced by permission of the author.

Somerset Maugham, 'The Verger'. Reproduced by permission of A P Watt on behalf of The Royal Literary Fund.

Bill Naughton, 'A Good Smile' from Goalkeeper's Revenge and Other Stories by Bill Naughton reprinted by permission of Peters Fraser & Dunlop (www.petersfraserdunlop.com) on behalf of the Estate of Bill Naughton.

R K Narayan, 'Gateman's Gift' from Malgudi Days. Reproduced with permission of Legal Heirs of R K Narayan.

Every effort has been made to trace copyright holders and to obtain their permission for the use of copyright material. The publisher apologises for any errors or omissions made, and would be grateful if notified of any corrections that should be incorporated in future reprints or editions of this book.

Foreword

The job market today, is a dynamic and challenging place for young people graduating from our educational institutions. While the number of job seekers is on the rise, so are the employment opportunities available to them. However, many employers say that they are unable to find suitable candidates for the jobs they have. Of the candidates who appear for campus interviews every year, only about thirty percent are selected for employment. This does not mean that students are poorly equipped with technical knowledge and skills. On the contrary, many are adequately qualified in this area. The problem is that they lack proficiency in English and the soft skills necessary for professionals today.

The need to equip graduating students with skills essential for the workplace has become an urgent concern. Many governments worldwide have set up committees to examine this problem and come up with recommendations. The Secretary's Commission on Achieving Necessary Skills (SCANS) report in the US, for example, is one of many reports, which emphasises the need to develop essential employability skills such as communication, listening, willingness to learn, teamwork, and so on.

Many universities and colleges have started thinking about introducing courses in soft skills. Some have already prepared materials and trained teachers to offer soft skills at the postgraduate and undergraduate levels. But what the teachers and students feel about the course is important to consider. In fact, to know what others feel is a soft skill. It is in this context that Dr S P Dhanavel, who has been trained by Scope International in collaboration with the Electronics Corporation of Tamilnadu, has written this timely textbook, *English and Soft Skills*. This is a book aimed at developing the soft skills of students at the undergraduate level. It is suitable for different classroom situations and fits in with the syllabuses and examination patterns of various universities.

Dr Dhanavel's book gives scope for students to work on a set of ten interlinked soft skills: listening, teamwork, emotional intelligence, assertiveness, learning to learn, problem solving, attending interviews, adaptability, non-verbal communication and written communication. Students can learn these skills through a number of activities: pair work, group work, role play, discussion, presentation, storytelling, assignments, etc. The course book will help students to enter the job market with confidence and the ability to work effectively in the professions of their choice.

I am confident that educational administrators, teachers, and students will welcome this book as they will find it a valuable resource, which will enable them to produce employable graduates.

(Dr P Mannar Jawahar)

Preface

Learning and teaching, in that order, have been my passion for years. Learning about what is useful to my students has been my guiding principle. As a result, I read newspapers and magazines which give tips to students on how to perform well academically and professionally. Thus, I became interested in soft skills over ten years ago. The Electronics Corporation of Tamilnadu (ELCOT), which is a nodal agency for promoting interaction between industry and the government, organised training programmes in soft skills for the teachers of Tamilnadu. After attending one of the programmes, I developed a deeper understanding of the role, importance and teaching of soft skills. Then the Academic Staff College of Bharathiar University gave me a golden chance to share my views on soft skills at a 'Refresher Course on Employability Skills' for college teachers. I also wrote articles on soft skills and presented them at the annual conferences of the English Language Teachers' Association of India (ELTAI).

All these efforts have now taken the shape of this textbook on English and soft skills. I have been fortunate to have had the good will and best wishes of my colleagues and friends. I thank everyone who has encouraged me to think anew and break fresh ground with this book.

I am deeply indebted to Mr Uma Shankar, the former Managing Director, ELCOT, Mr Chandrasekar, Head, Training, Mrs Hema Narayanan, Coordinator, and Mr Celestine Paulraj, Trainer of Scope International, for their seriousousness and commitment to educating teachers in the area of soft skills training.

I am grateful to the following members of Anna University—the Vice-Chancellor, the Registrar, the Dean, CEG Campus and the Chairman, Faculty of Science and Humanities—for their support, encouragement and permission to bring out this book.

My sincere thanks are due to our Vice-Chancellor, Dr P Mannar Jawahar, for his kind foreword to the book.

I would like to thank my colleagues: Dr Premalatha Rajan, Professor, Dr K Elango, Professor, Dr T Shrimathy Venkatalakshmi, Assistant Professor, Dr S Soundiraraj, Assistant Professor, Mr P Sadagopan, Lecturer (SG) Dr Veena Selvam, Lecturer, Dr Stars Jasmine, Lecturer, and all the supporting staff for their cooperation and understanding.

I would like to express my gratitude to Dr Shreesh Chaudhury, Professor of English, Indian Institute of Technology, Madras. His words of advice and motivation have been of great support to me. Similarly, Dr R Palanivel, Professor and Head, Department of English, Bharathiar University, Coimbatore, has provided me with a sounding board for my ideas, and has guided me with his knowledge and wisdom. The blessings of Dr F Abdul Rahim, Professor and Head, Department of English, Annamalai University, Annamalainagar, have always been a source of strength to me. I would like to add to this list, my former doctoral student and now colleague, Dr S Kumaran, for his help.

I would like to thank Mr Wilfred Fernandez and Mr Tapan Das of Orient Blackswan for helping me bring this book to publication. Finally, my thanks to Ms Deepa Kilambi for her editorial input.

S P Dhanavel

How to Use this Book

English and Soft Skills is a learner-oriented book intended to help students acquire and practice soft skills. The book is divided into ten units with each unit focusing on a separate soft skill. These skills have been introduced through a variety of short stories from across the world. However, as no skill can be learnt in isolation, ideas and activities may overlap from one chapter to another. All the units in the book follow a similar structure to ensure consistency and predictability, so that the learner can proceed from one chapter to the next, with ease.

Many activities have been included in the book for the students to learn and practice both language and soft skills inside the classroom. Pair work, group discussion, role play, presentation, storytelling, listening, writing and exploring proverbs and their relationship to work skills, are some attractive features of this book. They encourage the active involvement of the students in learning. The role of the teacher is to facilitate and help students to acquire these skills.

To the teacher

Your role is that of a facilitator rather than a teacher. You need to guide and help the students complete the activities in the book. Since the activities are many and varied, it is important that you go through the material in advance and prepare yourself for the classroom. You could suggest additional activities to your students. However, if the activities need preparation on the part of your students, let them know well in advance.

Stories are an integral part of language learning. That is why eight stories, a prose piece and an extract from a novel have been chosen to form the backbone of this book. In addition to helping students acquire vocabulary and other important aspects of language, the stories in the book establish a framework within which students can understand essential aspects of the soft skills they will require when they start working. To maximise the learning of students, you can ask them to read the stories in the 'Further reading' section and then give each student a minute or two to tell the story in the class. Besides helping students build up their confidence levels, storytelling is a skill that is often required in social interactions. Devote five or ten minutes of every class to storytelling.

Encourage your students to discuss issues and ask questions. Listen to their questions, clarify their doubts and provide them with the guidance and reassurance that will help them to speak out. Be a good listener and communicator so as to motivate your students. They will appreciate your efforts.

To the student

Many of you may have the impression that if you do well in your examinations you are sure to land your dream job. So you focus your attention on studying hard and getting high marks. But reality demands more than high marks. In the job market, it is your soft skills, also known as, employable skills, which decide your professional life. Many employers and placement professionals say that students passing out from colleges and schools are not employable because they lack these skills. Then you may ask, 'How do I make myself employable?'

This book is a practical answer to your question. It will help you understand what employers look for when you attend interviews and what you have to do when you join an organisation. It presents the soft skills you require through short stories which you will enjoy reading and thinking about. It also gives you enough opportunities to learn, practice and hone your soft skills inside and outside the classroom. Work hard to complete the tasks and assignments in the book and you are certain to benefit from it.

Do bring your book to class every day. It will also be useful to bring a portable dictionary with you, which will help you with vocabulary and other language activities. Vocabulary and language development are important for all students. Maintain a notebook for your writing activities. It will also serve as a record of the skills and qualities you learn through the course. Make use of the section on further reading to enhance your reading skills and improve upon your soft skills. Submit assignments to your teacher regularly and check your soft skills honestly at the end of every unit. Build up team spirit in the class by working with each other, participating in discussions and role plays, and sharing ideas. Work at developing your skills with a positive attitude and a determination of purpose and you are sure to stand a very good chance in the job market.

Please do not hesitate to contact the author to give your feedback or for any information or assistance. He can be reached at *dhanavelsp@yahoo.co.in*.

1. Listening Skills

Leading up to the story

Discuss these questions in groups of four or five. The group leader may then present the answers to the class.

1. What is the role of a bank?
2. Why do some banks fail and collapse? Think of economic events in the world that have contributed to the failure of banks.
3. Name some successful and unsuccessful banks.

The boy who broke the bank

Read the story by Ruskin Bond. Then answer the questions that follow.

Nathu grumbled to himself as he swept the steps of the Pipalnagar Bank, owned by Seth Govind Ram. He used the small broom hurriedly and carelessly, and the dust, after rising in a cloud above his head settled down again on the steps. As Nathu was banging his pan against a dustbin, Sitaram, the washerman's son, passed by.

Sitaram was on his delivery round. He had a bundle of freshly pressed clothes balanced on his head.

'Don't raise such dust!' he called out to Nathu. 'Are you annoyed because they are still refusing to pay you an extra two rupees a month?'

'I don't wish to talk about it,' complained the sweeper boy. 'I haven't even received my regular pay. And this is the twentieth of the month. Who would think a bank would hold up a poor man's salary? As soon as I get my money, I'm off! Not another week I work in this place.' And Nathu banged the pan against the dustbin several times, just to emphasise his point and give himself confidence.

'Well, I wish you luck,' said Sitaram. 'I'll keep a lookout for any jobs that might suit you.' And he plodded barefoot along the road, the big bundle of clothes hiding most of his head and shoulders.

At the fourth home he visited, Sitaram heard the lady of the house mention that she was in need of a sweeper. Tying his bundle together, he said, 'I know of a sweeper boy who's looking for work. He can start from next month. He's with the bank just now but they aren't giving him his pay, and he wants to leave.'

'Is that so?' said Mrs Srivastava. 'Well, tell him to come and see me tomorrow.'

And Sitaram, glad that he had been of service to both a customer and his friend, hoisted his bag on his shoulders and went his way.

Mrs Srivastava had to do some shopping. She gave instructions to the *ayah* about looking after the baby, and told the cook not to be late with the mid-day meal. Then she set out for the Pipalnagar marketplace, to make her customary tour of the cloth shops.

A large, shady tamarind tree grew at one end of the bazaar, and it was here that Mrs Srivastava found her friend Mrs Bhushan sheltering from the heat. Mrs Bhushan was fanning herself with a large handkerchief. She complained of the summer which, she affirmed was definitely the hottest in the history of Pipalnagar. She then showed Mrs Srivastava a sample of the cloth she was going to buy, and for five minutes they discussed its shade, texture, and design. Having exhausted this topic, Mrs Srivastava said, 'Do you know, my dear, that Seth Govind Ram's bank can't even pay its employees? Only this morning I heard a complaint from their sweeper, who hasn't received his wages for over a month!'

'Shocking!' remarked Mrs Bhushan. 'If they can't pay the sweeper they must be in a bad way. None of the others could be getting paid either.'

She left Mrs Srivastava at the tamarind tree and went in search of her husband, who was sitting in front of Kamal Kishore's photographic shop, talking to the owner.

'So there you are!' cried Mrs Bhushan. 'I've been looking for you for almost an hour. Where did you disappear?'

'Nowhere,' replied Mr Bhushan. 'Had you remained stationary in one shop, I might have found you. But you go from one shop to another, like a bee in a flower garden.'

'Don't start grumbling. The heat is trying enough. I don't know what's happening to Pipalnagar. Even the bank's about to go bankrupt.'

'What's that?' said Kamal Kishore, sitting up suddenly. 'Which bank?'

'Why the Pipalnagar bank, of course. I hear they have stopped paying employees. Don't tell me you have an account there, Mr Kishore?'

'No, but my neighbour has!' he exclaimed; and he called out over the low partition to the keeper of the barber shop next door. 'Deep Chand, have you heard the latest? The Pipalnagar Bank is about to collapse. You'd better get your money out as soon as you can!'

Deep Chand, who was cutting the hair of an elderly gentleman, was so startled that his hand shook and he nicked his customer's right ear. The customer yelped in pain and distress: pain, because of the cut and distress, because of the awful news he had just heard. With one side of his neck still unshaven, he sped across the road to the general merchant's store where there was a telephone. He dialled Seth Govind Ram's number. The Seth was not at home. Where was he, then? The Seth was holidaying in Kashmir. Oh, was that so? The elderly gentleman did not believe it. He hurried back to the barber's shop and told Deep Chand: 'The bird has flown! Seth Govind Ram has left town. Definitely, it means a collapse.' And then he dashed out of the shop, making a beeline for his office and chequebook.

The news spread through the bazaar with the rapidity of forest fire. From the general merchant's it travelled to the shop, circulated amongst the customers, and then spread with them in various directions, to the betel seller, the tailor, the free vendor, the jeweller, the beggar sitting on the pavement.

Old Ganpath, the beggar, had a crooked leg. He had been squatting on the pavement for years, calling for alms. In the evening someone would come with a barrow to take him away. He had never been known to walk. But now, on learning that the bank was about to collapse, Ganpath astonished everyone by leaping to his feet and actually running at top speed in the direction of the bank. It soon became known that he had a thousand rupees in savings!

Men stood in groups at street corners discussing the situation. Pipalnagar seldom had a crisis, seldom or never had floods, earthquakes or drought; and the imminent crash of the Pipalnagar Bank set everyone talking and speculating and rushing about in a frenzy. Some boasted of their farsightedness, congratulating themselves on having already taken out their money, or on never having put any in; others speculated on the reasons for the crash, putting it all down to excesses indulged in by Seth Govind Ram. The Seth had fled the State, said one. He had fled the country, said another. He was hiding in Pipalnagar, said a third. He had hanged himself from the tamarind tree, said a fourth, and had been found that morning by the sweeper boy.

By noon the small bank had gone through all its ready cash, and the harassed manager was in a dilemma. Emergency funds could only be obtained from another bank some thirty miles distant, and he wasn't sure he could persuade the crowd to wait until then. And there was no way of contacting Seth Govind Ram on his houseboat in Kashmir.

People were turned back from the counters and told to return the following day. They did not like the sound of that. And so they gathered outside, on the steps of the bank, shouting, 'Give us our money or we'll break in!' and 'Fetch the Seth, we know he's hiding in a safe deposit locker!' Mischief makers, who didn't have a paisa in the bank, joined the crowd and aggravated the mood. The manager stood at the door and tried to placate them. He declared that the bank had plenty of money but no immediate means of collecting it; he urged them to go home and come back the next day.

'We want it now!' chanted some of the crowd. 'Now, now, now!'

And a brick hurtled through the air and crashed through the plate glass window of the Pipalnagar Bank.

Nathu arrived next morning to sweep the steps of the bank. He saw the refuse and the broken glass and the stones cluttering the steps. Raising his hands in a gesture of horror and disgust he cried: 'Hooligans! Sons of donkeys! As though it isn't bad enough to be paid late, it seems my work has also to be increased!' He smote the steps with his broom scattering the refuse.

'Good morning, Nathu,' said the washerman's boy, getting down from his bicycle. 'Are you ready to take up a new job from the first of the next month? You'll have to I suppose, now that the bank is going out of business.'

'How's that?' said Nathu.

'Haven't you heard? Well, you'd better wait here until half the population of Pipalnagar arrives to claim their money.' And he waved cheerfully — he did not have a bank account—and sped away on his cycle.

Nathu went back to sweeping the steps, muttering to himself. When he had finished his work, he sat down on the highest step, to await the arrival of the manager. He was determined to get his pay.

'Who would have thought the bank would collapse!' he said to himself, and looked thoughtfully into the distance. 'I wonder how it could have happened...

Ruskin Bond

Understanding the story

Answer the following questions. Later you may discuss your answers in the class.

1. Who is Nathu?
2. Who is Sitaram?
3. What does Sitaram tell Mrs Srivatsava?
4. Mrs Srivatsava says, 'I heard a complaint from their sweeper.' Was it a correct understanding of what the sweeper had said?
5. How does Mrs Bhushan interpret Mrs Srivastava's statement?
6. Why does Mr Kishore speak to Deep Chand?
7. Why does the elderly gentleman rush to the general merchant's store? According to him what had Seth Govind Ram done?
8. How does the rumour spread from the photographer's shop?
9. What is interesting about the beggar?
10. How does the manager try to handle the angry customers?
11. What do people imagine about Seth Govind Ram?
12. Who or what really breaks the bank?

Understanding people

There are many characters who appear in the story. Group them as primary or secondary in the table below.

Primary characters	Secondary characters
1.	
2.	
3.	
4.	
5.	
6.	
7.	
8.	
9.	
10.	

Understanding places and events

The action of the story occurs in many places. Identify the places and events mentioned in the story and complete the table.

Places	Events
1.	
2.	
3.	
4.	
5.	

Vocabulary development

Meanings in context

Look up a dictionary and find the meanings of the words and phrases below, as they are used in the context of the story.

Words and phrases	Meanings
1. hold up	
2. plod	
3. bankrupt	
4. dash out	
5. rapidity	

6. barrow
7. imminent
8. farsighted
9. aggravated
10. refuse
11. clutter
12. smote

Noun suffixes

Look at the following words. They belong to a group of words called nouns, which are naming words.

confidence, rapidity, instruction, situation, direction, pavement, beggar, shopping, savings, arrival

These are formed by adding suffixes or word endings to other words. For example, *-ion* is added after *instruct* to form *instruction* and *-er* is added after *sweep* to form *sweeper.*

Match the suffixes with the words and make nouns.

	Word	Suffix	Noun
1.	urgent	– able	
2.	maintain	– ity	
3.	build	– ee	
4.	astonish	– tion	
5.	impede	– er	
6.	speculate	– ment	
7.	travel	– ance	
8.	pay	– ness	
9.	employ	– cy	
10.	farsighted	– ing	

Professionals and people

There are a number of words in the story which refer to various professionals and people who we meet in our daily life. These words end in *-er, -or, -ar* and *-ee,* for example, *sweeper, vendor, beggar* and *employee.*

Find other words in the story, which are similar to those in the example. You should be able to get at least ten words of this kind.

....

....

Using words accurately

'Pain' and 'distress' are two words used in the story with reference to the elderly gentleman, a customer of Deep Chand. Notice how Ruskin Bond distinguishes between the two words in terms of meaning.

'The customer yelped with pain and distress: pain, because of the cut and distress because of the awful news he had just heard.'

Can you think of other pairs of words with subtle differences in meaning and use them in sentences of your own?

Read the pairs of words below. Bring out the differences in meaning by using them in sentences of your own.

- joy and happiness
- sad and gloomy
- listen and hear
- speak and talk
- communicate and converse
- intelligent and clever

Thinking about soft skills

Discuss these questions in pairs and answer them briefly.

1. How is listening different from hearing?
2. Why is it important to listen?
3. Do you often find it difficult to listen properly? How can you overcome this difficulty?

Listening skills from the story

Listening is a facility that most living beings possess. While animals retain their listening ability long after babyhood, human beings seem to lose their capacity to listen as they grow older. Notice how many people are unable to listen to teachers in college classrooms and to colleagues and employers in workplaces.

When we were young we could communicate with people fairly easily. This is because we depended more on our non-verbal communication skills. But now that we are older there are so many things that interfere with our capacity to listen. What then should we do? When somebody speaks, we must listen. If we do not understand what a person says, we can ask questions to clarify our doubts. We must look beyond the words being spoken and try to understand what the person is thinking and feeling. In other words, we must learn to listen with empathy.

The sweeper boy in the story needs to get his salary but the manager does not care about the boy and his difficulties. On the other hand, the washerman's boy listens to his friend. He understands the sweeper boy's difficulties, empathises with him and actually starts looking for another job for his friend.

Mrs Srivastava develops her own mistaken understanding of the boy's intention to leave the bank. She casually shares her knowledge with her friend who in turn tells her husband, and thus the rumour of the collapse of the bank spreads like wildfire.

Thus the manager's inability to listen with empathy to the sweeper boy brings down the bank. There is unnecessary chaos leading to a law and order problem in the town.

Activity

1. **Five or six students can come to the front of the class and stand in a row. The teacher then whispers a message to one student. Now the student whispers the message to the next student and so on down the line until the last student, who speaks the message out aloud. The teacher then tells the class what the original message was.**

   The original message will be completely distorted!

   Messages are often distorted in this manner. In fact, the longer the chain, the worse the distortion. Effective listening and reduction in the length of the communication chain are the only solutions to this problem.

2. **Here is a poem on active listening. Read through it, and notice how the poet feels when people do not listen.**

Active Listening

When I ask you to listen to me,
and you start giving me advice,
you have not done what I asked.

When I ask that you listen to me,

and you begin to tell me why I shouldn't feel that way,
you are trampling on my feelings.

When I ask you listen to me,
and you feel you have to do something to solve my problems,
you have failed me, strange as that may seem.

Listen:
all that I ask is that you listen
not talk or do—just hear me.
When you do something for me,
that I need to do for myself,
you contribute to my feelings of inadequacy.

But when you accept as a simple fact
that I do feel what I feel, no matter how irrational,
then I can quit trying to convince you
and go about the business of understanding what's behind my feelings.

So please listen and just hear me,
and if you want to talk,
wait a minute for your turn—and I'll listen to you.

Anonymous

Answer the following questions.

1. Instead of listening to the poet, what does the person in the poem do?
2. Have you observed any other behaviour of people who don't listen to you?

Proverbs on listening skills

1. **Read the following proverbs from various countries about the importance of listening. Can you add a few more proverbs from your mother tongue or any other language? Which proverb do you like the most? Why? Share your views with the class.**

    a. Listening is the beginning of understanding.... Wisdom is the reward of a lifetime of listening.
    b. Listening requires more intelligence than speaking.
    c. To listen well is as powerful a means of influence as to talk well, and is as essential to all true conversation.
    d. Talk becomes an argument when one person stops listening.

e. Listening looks easy, but it is not simple. Every head is a world.
f. Who speaks sows; who listens reaps.
g. Eat what is cooked; listen to what is said.
h. Listen a hundred times; ponder a thousand times; speak once.
i. From listening comes wisdom and from speaking, repentance.
j. The wise man has long ears and a short tongue.

2. **Choose the proverb which best summarises the story and explain your choice to the class.**

3. **The proverbs in the previous exercise indicate that listening and speaking complement each other. Now write a paragraph of 150 words showing the connection between listening and speaking.**

Soft skills at the workplace

Discuss these questions in groups of four or five and share your answers with the class. Each group can choose one topic.

1. Why is it important to listen to our customers and clients?
2. How does listening help in developing good relations with people?
3. How is listening and understanding from another person's point of view important for a manager?
4. It is important to listen to every employee in the organisation, including those at the bottom of the hierarchy. Why?

Real life experience

In a paragraph of 150 words write about an instance when somebody did not listen to you and its consequence *or* when you did not listen well and its consequence.

Self-assessment

Read the following 'yes' or 'no' questions carefully. If your answer is YES, write 1. If your answer is NO, write 0.

	Questions	1 or 0
1.	Do you lean forward towards the speaker?	
2.	Do you face the speaker directly?	
3.	Do you maintain an open body position?	

4. Do you maintain an appropriate distance from the speaker?
5. Do you nod your head frequently to indicate that you are listening?
6. Do you mirror facial expressions (e.g. joy when somebody is happy)?
7. Do you adjust your body position without drawing attention?
8. Do you keep sustained and direct eye contact with your speaker?
9. Do you encourage and invite somebody to speak to you?
10. Do you encourage the speaker to continue to talk?
11. Do you give a person time to speak?
12. Do you show interest in the other person during a conversation?
13. Do you keep quiet in order to be attentive to your speaker?
14. Do you ask open-ended questions to keep the conversation going and to elicit further information?
15. Do you indicate that you are with, and not against, the speaker?
16. Do you rephrase the comments of your speaker for better understanding?
17. Do you share similar experiences with the speaker?
18. Do you identify the emotions behind the words of your speaker?
19. Do you pay attention to the person's emotions as well as the meaning of the words used?
20. Do you summarise the main points of the speaker?
21. Do you listen with an open mind?

If your score is between 15–21, you have excellent listening skills. If your score is less than 15, you have to improve your listening skills.

Further reading

Here are a few more stories by Ruskin Bond. Read them and, if possible, discuss them in the class.

1. The Eyes Have It
2. The Meeting Pool
3. The Thief
4. My Eccentric Guests
5. The Woman on Platform 8

2. Teamwork Skills

Leading up to the story

Discuss these questions in groups of four or five. The group leader then may present the answers to the class.

1. What kind of work do you find boring and tiresome?
2. What were the things you enjoyed doing when you were a child?
3. What was one task you had to do but hated to do?

Whitewashing the fence

Read the story taken from Mark Twain's novel, *The Adventures of Tom Sawyer*. Then answer the questions that follow.

Saturday morning was come, and all the summer world was bright and fresh, and brimming with life. There was a song in every heart; and if the heart was young the music issued at the lips. There was cheer in every face and a spring in every step. The locust-trees were in bloom and the fragrance of the blossoms filled the air. Cardiff Hill, beyond the village and above it, was green with vegetation and it lay just far enough away to seem a Delectable Land, dreamy, reposeful, and inviting.

Tom appeared on the sidewalk with a bucket of whitewash and a long-handled brush. He surveyed the fence, and all gladness left him and a deep melancholy settled down upon his spirit. Thirty yards of board fence nine feet high. Life to him seemed hollow, and existence but a burden. Sighing, he dipped his brush and passed it along the topmost plank; repeated the operation; did it again; compared the insignificant whitewashed streak with the far-reaching continent of unwhitewashed fence, and sat down on a tree-box discouraged. Jim came skipping out at the gate with a tin pail, and singing 'Buffalo Gals'. Bringing water from the town pump had always been hateful work in Tom's eyes, before, but now it did not strike him so. He remembered that there was company at the pump. White, *mulatto, and **negro boys and girls were always there waiting their turns, resting, trading playthings, quarrelling, fighting,

---

* Mulatto A person with one black parent and one white parent.

** Negro An offensive, old fashioned usage which refers to a black person.

skylarking. And he remembered that although the pump was only a hundred and fifty yards off, Jim never got back with a bucket of water under an hour—and even then somebody generally had to go after him. Tom said:

'Say, Jim, I'll fetch the water if you'll whitewash some.'

Jim shook his head and said:

'Can't, Mars Tom. Ole missis, she tole me I got to go an' git dis water an' not stop foolin' roun' wid anybody. She say she spec' Mars Tom gwine to ax me to whitewash, an' so she tole me go 'long an' 'tend to my own business—she 'lowed *she'd* 'tend to de whitewashin'.'

'Oh, never you mind what she said, Jim. That's the way she always talks. Gimme the bucket—I won't be gone only a minute. SHE won't ever know.'

'Oh, I dasn't, Mars Tom. Ole missis she'd take an' tar de head off'n me. 'Deed she would.'

'*She!* She never licks anybody—whacks 'em over the head with her thimble—and who cares for that, I'd like to know. She talks awful, but talk don't hurt—anyways it don't if she don't cry. Jim, I'll give you a marvel. I'll give you a white alley!'

Jim began to waver.

'White alley, Jim! And it's a bully taw.'

'My! Dat's a mighty gay marvel, I tell you! But Mars Tom I's powerful 'fraid ole missis—'

'And besides, if you will I'll show you my sore toe.'

Jim was only human—this attraction was too much for him. He put down his pail, took the white alley, and bent over the toe with absorbing interest while the bandage was being unwound. In another moment he was flying down the street with his pail and a tingling rear, Tom was whitewashing with vigour, and Aunt Polly was retiring from the field with a slipper in her hand and triumph in her eye. But Tom's energy did not last. He began to think of the fun he had planned for this day, and his sorrows multiplied. Soon the free boys would come tripping along on all sorts of delicious expeditions, and they would make a world of fun of him for having to work—the very thought of it burnt him like fire. He got out his worldly wealth and examined it—bits of toys, marbles, and trash; enough to buy an exchange of WORK, maybe, but not half enough to buy so much as half an hour of pure freedom. So he returned his straitened means to his pocket, and gave up the idea of trying to buy the boys. At this dark and hopeless moment an inspiration burst upon him! Nothing less than a great, magnificent inspiration.

He took up his brush and went tranquilly to work. Ben Rogers hove in sight presently —the very boy, of all boys, whose ridicule he had been dreading. Ben's gait was the hop-skip-and-jump—proof enough that his heart was light and his anticipations high. He was eating an apple, and giving a long, melodious whoop, at intervals, followed by a deep-toned ding-dong-dong, ding-dong-dong, for he was personating a steamboat. As he drew near, he slackened speed, took the middle of the street, leaned far over to star-board and rounded to ponderously and with laborious pomp and circumstance —for he was personating the *Big Missouri*, and considered himself to be drawing nine feet of water. He was boat and captain and engine-bells combined, so he had to imagine himself standing on his own hurricane-deck giving the orders and executing them:

'Stop her, sir! Ting-a-ling-ling!' The headway ran almost out, and he drew up slowly toward the sidewalk.

'Ship up to back! Ting-a-ling-ling!' His arms straightened and stiffened down his sides.

'Set her back on the stabboard! Ting-a-ling-ling! Chow! ch-chow-wow! Chow!' His right hand, meantime, describing stately circles—for it was representing a forty-foot wheel.

'Let her go back on the labboard! Ting-a-ling-ling! Chow-ch-chow-chow!' The left hand began to describe circles.

'Stop the stabboard! Ting-a-ling-ling! Stop the labboard! Come ahead on the stabboard! Stop her! Let your outside turn over slow! Ting-a-ling-ling! Chow-ow-ow! Get out that head-line! *lively* now! Come—out with your spring-line—what're you about there! Take a turn round that stump with the bight of it! Stand by that stage, now —let her go! Done with the engines, sir! Ting-a-ling-ling!'

'*Sh't! s'h't! sh't!*' (trying the gauge-cocks).

Tom went on whitewashing—paid no attention to the steamboat. Ben stared a moment and then said: 'Hi- Yi! *you're* up a stump, ain't you!'

No answer. Tom surveyed his last touch with the eye of an artist, then he gave his brush another gentle sweep and surveyed the result, as before. Ben ranged up alongside of him. Tom's mouth watered for the apple, but he stuck to his work. Ben said:

'Hello, old chap, you got to work, hey?'

Tom wheeled suddenly and said:

'Why, it's you, Ben! I warn't noticing.'

'Say—I'm going in a-swimming, I am. Don't you wish you could? But of course you'd druther *work*—wouldn't you? Course you would!'

Tom contemplated the boy a bit, and said:

'What do you call work?'

'Why, ain't *that* work?'

Tom resumed his whitewashing, and answered carelessly:

'Well, maybe it is, and maybe it ain't. All I know, is, it suits Tom Sawyer.'

'Oh come, now, you don't mean to let on that you *like* it?'

The brush continued to move.

'Like it? Well, I don't see why I oughtn't to like it. Does a boy get a chance to whitewash a fence every day?'

That put the thing in a new light. Ben stopped nibbling his apple. Tom swept his brush daintily back and forth—stepped back to note the effect—added a touch here and there—criticised the effect again—Ben watching every move and getting more and more interested, more and more absorbed. Presently he said:

'Say, Tom, let *me* whitewash a little.'

Tom considered, was about to consent; but he altered his mind:

'No—no—I reckon it wouldn't hardly do, Ben. You see, Aunt Polly's awful particular about this fence—right here on the street, you know—but if it was the back fence I wouldn't mind and *she* wouldn't. Yes, she's awful particular about this fence; it's got to be done very careful; I reckon there ain't one boy in a thousand, maybe two thousand, that can do it the way it's got to be done."

'No—is that so? Oh come, now—lemme just try. Only just a little—I'd let *you,* if you was me, Tom.'

'Ben, I'd like to, honest injun; but Aunt Polly—well, Jim wanted to do it, but she wouldn't let him; Sid wanted to do it, and she wouldn't let Sid. Now don't you see how I'm fixed? If you was to tackle this fence and anything was to happen to it—'

'Oh, shucks, I'll be just as careful. Now lemme try. Say—I'll give you the core of my apple.'

'Well, here—No, Ben, now don't. I'm afeard—'

'I'll give you *all* of it!'

Tom gave up the brush with reluctance in his face, but alacrity in his heart. And while the late steamer *Big Missouri* worked and sweated in the sun, the retired artist sat on a barrel in the shade close by, dangled his legs, munched his apple, and planned the slaughter of more innocents. There was no lack of material; boys happened along every little while; they came to jeer, but remained to whitewash. By the time Ben was fagged out, Tom had traded the next chance to Billy Fisher for a kite, in good repair; and when he played out, Johnny Miller bought in for a dead rat and a string to swing it with — and so on, and so on, hour after hour. And when the middle of the afternoon came, from being a poor poverty-stricken boy in the morning, Tom was literally rolling in wealth. He had besides the things before mentioned, twelve marbles, part of a jews-harp, a piece of blue bottle-glass to look through, a spool cannon, a key that wouldn't unlock anything, a fragment of chalk, a glass stopper of a decanter, a tin soldier, a couple of tadpoles, six fire-crackers, a kitten with only one eye, a brass doorknob, a dog-collar—but no dog —the handle of a knife, four pieces of orange-peel, and a dilapidated old window sash.

He had had a nice, good, idle time all the while—plenty of company—and the fence had three coats of whitewash on it! If he hadn't run out of whitewash he would have bankrupted every boy in the village.

Tom said to himself that it was not such a hollow world, after all. He had discovered a great law of human action, without knowing it—namely, that in order to make a man or a boy covet a thing, it is only necessary to make the thing difficult to attain. If he had been a great and wise philosopher, like the writer of this book, he would now have comprehended that Work consists of whatever a body is *obliged* to do, and that Play consists of whatever a body is not obliged to do. And this would help him to understand why constructing artificial flowers or performing on a tread-mill is work, while rolling ten-pins or climbing Mont Blanc is only amusement. There are wealthy gentlemen in England who drive four-horse passenger-coaches twenty or thirty miles on a daily line, in the summer, because the privilege costs them considerable money; but if they were offered wages for the service, that would turn it into work and then they would resign.

The boy mused awhile over the substantial change which had taken place in his worldly circumstances, and then wended toward headquarters to report.

Mark Twain

Understanding the story

Answer the following questions. Later you may discuss your answers in the class.

1. Describe the mood expressed in the opening lines of the story.
2. How was Tom feeling on that Saturday morning? Why was he feeling that way?
3. What happened when Jim started to whitewash the fence?
4. Is Tom afraid of Aunt Polly? Give reasons for your answer.
5. How does Tom succeed in getting Ben to whitewash the fence?
6. How did Tom manage to become wealthy by the afternoon? Mention some of the things that made him wealthy.
7. How does the author differentiate between work and play?
8. What 'great law of human action' did Tom discover?

Understanding people

There are many characters who appear in the story. Group them as primary or secondary in the table below.

Primary characters	Secondary characters
1.	
2.	
3.	

Understanding ideas

The author mentions these two ideas in the story. Find examples from the story which explain each idea.

Ideas	Examples
1. In order to make a man or a boy covet a thing, it is only necessary to make the thing difficult to attain.	
2. Work consists of whatever a body is *obliged* to do, and play consists of whatever a body is not obliged to do.	

Vocabulary development

Meanings in context

Look up a dictionary and find the meanings of the words and phrases below, as they are used in the story.

	Words and phrases	Meanings
1.	delectable	
2.	insignificant	
3.	triumph	
4.	expedition	
5.	inspiration	
6.	hove in sight	
7.	anticipation	
8.	ponderous	
9.	range up	
10.	contemplate	
11.	happen along	
12.	covet	
13.	attain	
14.	muse	

Adjectives

Short adjectives

Look at these words. They belong to a group of words called adjectives, which are describing words.

old, long, soft, great, quiet, big, gentle, clean, brave, low, plain

These are simple words with one syllable. They have comparative and superlative forms. We get the comparative form by adding *–er* and the superlative form by adding *-est*. Thus, *old* + *-er* = older, and *old* + *-est* = oldest.

Write the comparative and superlative forms of the adjectives listed above and use them in sentences of your own.

For example: Tom is cleverer than the other boys. In fact, he is the cleverest of them all.

Adjectival suffixes

Here is another list of words which are adjectives.

comfortable, heavy, peaceful, meaningless, tired, destructive, dreamy, inviting, hopeless

They are formed by adding suffixes or word endings to the main words. For example, comfort + *-able* = *comfortable*, and *peace* + *-ful* = *peaceful*.

Form adjectives by adding suitable suffixes to the words below and complete the table.

	Words	Suffixes	Adjectives
1.	silence	–al	
2.	technique	–ous	
3.	nature	–ic	
4.	triumph	–ive	
5.	hero	–t	
6.	attraction	–ly	
7.	vigour	–y	
8.	horror	–ical	
9.	anger	–less	
10.	afford	-ent/-ant	
11.	purpose	-able / -ible	
12.	life	-ful	

WORDS USED AS NOUNS AND ADJECTIVES

Look at the following words: *hollow, right, rich* and *professional*.
These words can be used both as adjectives and nouns. For example, *hollow* is an adjective in the first sentence and a noun in the second sentence.

- It was not such a *hollow* world after all.
- He hid himself in a *hollow* in the ground.

Make sentences of your own using the other words above as adjectives and nouns.

Thinking about soft skills

Work in pairs and discuss these questions.

1. What is a team?
2. What are the skills required to work in a team?
3. How will you develop these skills in yourself?

Teamwork skills from the story

Mark Twain tells the story of how Tom Sawyer manages to get out of doing a task set by his Aunt Polly as a punishment for disobeying her the day before. Tom is a bright and energetic young boy who has been condemned to whitewash a fence on a lovely summer's day. He knows that all his friends will be playing and enjoying themselves whereas he himself will have to work. But Tom's unhappiness does not last, because he comes up with a wonderful idea to solve his problem. The rest of the story is about how Tom Sawyer uses his intelligence to create a team of willing painters to whitewash the fence for him. Thus Tom turns a dreary and lonely task into an enjoyable one. In the end the work gets done and the fence ends up with not one, but three coats of paint! This was possible because Tom Sawyer unknowingly harnessed the benefits of teamwork for his own ends.

In this story, Tom is both funny and endearing. We cannot remain angry with him for tricking his friends because he does it out of innocence rather than meanness. In fact we laugh at his cleverness and enjoy the joke. But we would not feel the same if an adult indulges in trickery.

Work in groups and discuss the following situation.

Imagine that the supervisor in your office has set your team an important but not very interesting task. As the team leader, what would you do to help your team accomplish this task?

Activity

It is important to develop the ability to work as a team in order to function efficiently in the workplace. As employees of a company, we have to believe in the company's vision and work toward a common goal even if we disagree with some procedures or dislike the people involved. We must find ways to resolve emotional problems and disagreements so that the goals of the organisation are achieved. The best way to acquire teamwork skills is to start working with others who are different from you in ability, language, culture or life style.

Here are some activities you can participate in to develop your teamwork skills.

1. Form groups of three, four, or five to complete classroom learning tasks. Change the members of the group as frequently as possible.
2. Form a group e-mail id for the entire class, including the teachers who handle various subjects. Every student and teacher may share information through this email id. This can be maintained for a long time, so that students and teachers can keep in touch with each other.
3. Form groups when you need to work on presentations. Group members can be given tasks such as collecting information, analysing data, preparing power point slides, etc.
4. Organise group discussions on various topics.

Proverbs on teamwork skills

1. **Read the following proverbs from various countries about the importance of teamwork. Can you add a few more proverbs from your mother tongue or any other language? Which proverb do you like the most? Why? Share your views with the class.**

   a. United we stand, divided we fall.
   b. Two heads are better than one.
   c. Many hands make light work.
   d. Many hands can shatter stout walls.
   e. Gnats, in great numbers, can beat an elephant.
   f. Sticks in a bundle are unbreakable.
   g. Every spark adds to the fire.
   h. A monk cannot shave his own head.
   i. A single tree cannot make a forest.
   j. When a husband and wife agree with each other, they can dry up the ocean with buckets.

2. Choose the proverb which best summarises the story and explain your choice to the class.

3. Using the word TEAM as an acronym which stands for 'Together Everyone Achieves More', write a paragraph of 150 words on the importance of cooperation and collaboration.

Soft skills at the workplace

Discuss these questions in groups of four or five and share your answers with the class. Each group can choose one topic.

1. If you want to carry out an operation against a competitor in business, how will you achieve unity and team spirit within your group and in your company?
2. How do individual habits help or hinder working in teams?
3. How will you handle a situation when a team member does not report for work?
4. At higher levels of management, decision making is always a matter of life and death for a company. Discuss.
5. When a team is divided on certain issues, how will you bring about unity among the team members?

Real life experience

You may have watched games or been part of organising functions and special events held. Choose any one event and write about how teams, groups, and committees contribute to the success of the programme.

Self-assessment

Read the following 'yes' or 'no' questions carefully. If your answer is YES, write 1. If your answer is NO, write 0.

	Questions	1 or 0
1.	Do you believe in working towards a common goal?	
2.	Do you respond to the ideas of others positively?	
3.	Do you feel happy to work with others?	
4.	Do you appreciate others for their contribution?	
5.	Do you delegate responsibility to others?	
6.	Do you mentor your friends and group members?	
7.	Do you trust others?	

8. Do you help others achieve their individual goals?
9. Do you involve others in decision making?
10. Do you take responsibility for all your actions?
11. Do you share recognition and rewards with others?
12. Do you identify talents and nurture them?
13. Do you help others with difficult tasks or situations?
14. Do you network with people and maintain contacts?
15. Do you use your friendships with people ethically?
16. Do you generate enthusiasm and energy in people around you?
17. Do you offer constructive feedback to others?
18. Do you resolve conflicts?
19. Do you bring people together?
20. Do you pay sincere and timely attention to others?
21. Do you have a positive attitude to life, people and work?

If your score is between 15–21, you have excellent teamwork skills. If your score is less than 15, you have to improve your team skills.

Further reading

You can read, *The Adventures of Tom Sawyer* by Mark Twain for other interesting episodes involving Tom Sawyer and his family and friends. Later you may discuss the book in the class.

Here are some more novels for you to read.

1. *The Adventures of Huckleberry Finn*, Mark Twain
2. *The Adventures of Robinson Crusoe*, Daniel Defoe
3. *Swami and Friends*, R K Narayan

3. Emotional Intelligence Skills

Leading up to the story

Discuss these questions in groups of four or five. The group leader may then present the answers to the class.

1. Why do people go to banks?
2. When do we close a bank account?
3. What was your experience of opening a savings bank account?

My financial career

Read the prose piece by Stephen Leacock. Then answer the questions that follow.

When I go into a bank I get nervous. The clerks make me nervous; the little windows at the counters make me nervous; the sight of the money makes me nervous; everything makes me nervous.

The moment I go through the door of a bank and attempt to do business there, I become an irresponsible fool. I knew this before I went in, but my salary had been raised to fifty six dollars a month and I felt that the bank was the only place for it.

So I walked in with dragging feet and looked shyly round at the clerks. I had an idea that a person about to open an account was obliged to consult the manager.

I went up to a counter marked 'Accountant'. The Accountant was a tall, cool fellow. The very sight of him made me nervous. My voice was deep and hollow.

'Can I see the manager?' I said, and added solemnly, 'alone.' I don't know why I said 'alone.'

'Certainly,' said the accountant, and fetched him.

The manager was a grave, calm man. I held my fifty-six dollars clutched in a screwed-up ball in my pocket.

'Are you the manager?' I said. God knows I didn't doubt it.

'Yes,' he said.

'Can I see you,' I asked, 'alone?' I didn't want to say 'alone' again, but without it the thing seemed obvious. The manager looked at me in some alarm. He felt that I had a terrible secret to reveal.

'Come in here,' he said, and led the way to a private room. He turned the key in the lock.

'We are safe from interruption here,' he said: 'sit down.'

We both sat down and looked at each other. I found no voice to speak.

'You are one of Pinkerton's men, I suppose,' he said.

He had gathered from my mysterious manner that I was a detective. I knew what he was thinking, and it made me worse.

'No, not from Pinkerton's,' I said, seeming to suggest that I came from a rival agency.

'To tell the truth,' I went on, as if I had been tempted to lie about it, 'I am not a detective at all. I have come to open an account. I intend to keep all my money in this bank.'

The manager looked relieved but still serious; he concluded now that I was a son of Baron Rothschild or a young Gould.

'A large account, I suppose,' he said.

'Fairly large,' I whispered. 'I propose to deposit fifty-six dollars now and fifty dollars a month regularly.'

The manager got up and opened the door. He called to the accountant.

'Mr. Montgomery,' he said unkindly loud, 'this gentleman is opening an account. He will deposit fifty-six dollars. Good morning.'

I rose.

A big iron door stood open at the side of the room.

'Good morning,' I said, and stepped into the safe.

'Come out,' said the manager coldly, and showed me the other way.

I went up to the accountant's counter and pushed the ball of money at him with a sudden, quick movement as if I were doing a conjuring trick.

My face was pale as death.

'Here,' I said, 'deposit it.' The tone of the words seemed to mean, 'Let us do this painful thing while we are in mood for it.'

He took the money and gave it to another clerk.

He made me write the sum on a piece of paper and sign my name in a book. I no longer knew what I was doing. The bank was going round and round before my eyes.

'Is it deposited?' I asked in a hollow, vibrating voice.

'It is,' said the accountant.

'Then I want to draw a cheque.'

My idea was to draw out six dollars of it for present use. Someone gave me a cheque book through a little window and someone else began telling me how to write it out. The people in the bank had the impression that I was a millionaire who had something wrong with him. I wrote something on the cheque and thrust it in at the clerk. He looked at it.

'What! Are you drawing it all out again?' he asked in surprise. Then I realized that I had written fifty-six instead of six. I was too far gone to reason now. I had a feeling that it was impossible to explain the thing. All the clerks had stopped writing to look at me.

Reckless with misery, I made up my mind.

'Yes the whole thing.'

'You withdraw your money from the bank?'

'Every cent of it.'

'Are you not going to deposit any more?' said the clerk, astonished.

'Never.'

A foolish hope struck me that they might think something had insulted me while I was writing the cheque and that I had changed my mind. I made a wretched attempt to look like a man with a fearfully quick temper.

The clerk prepared to pay the money.

'How will you have it?' he said.

'What?'

'How will you have it?'

'Oh,'—I caught his meaning and answered without even trying to think,—'in fifties.'

He gave me a fifty dollar bill.

'And the six?' he asked dryly.

'In sixes,' I said.

He gave it to me and I rushed out.

As the big door swung behind me I caught the echo of a roar of laughter that went up to the ceiling of the bank. Since then I bank no more. I keep my money in cash in my trousers pocket and my savings in silver dollars in a sock.

Stephen Leacock

Understanding the story

Answer the following questions. Later you may discuss your answers in the class.

1. What makes the narrator feel nervous in a bank?
2. How does the accountant help the narrator in the beginning?
3. What prevents the narrator from telling the manager his purpose clearly?
4. How does the manager's behaviour change when he learns that the narrator wants to open an account with fifty-six dollars?
5. Why does the narrator deposit fifty-six dollars and then want to withdraw six dollars?

6. How did the narrator end up withdrawing all his money?
7. Who benefited from the transaction, the bank or the customer?
8. Do you think the story is imaginary or real?
9. What adjectives can you use to describe the narrator?
10. What will happen to the bank if it receives many customers of this kind every day?

Understanding people

There are many characters who appear in the story. Group them as primary or secondary in the table below

	Primary characters	Secondary characters
1.		
2.		
3.		
4.		

Understanding emotions

The narrator and the people in the bank experience a variety of emotions. Make a list of the characters, the emotions each one experiences and the effect of each emotion on the other characters.

	Character	Emotions	Effect
1.			
2.			
3.			
4.			
5.			

Vocabulary development

Meanings in context

Look up a dictionary and find the meanings of the words and phrases below, as they are used in the context of the story.

Words and phrases	Meanings
1. dragging	
2. hollow	
3. solemnly	
4. clutched	
5. turn in	
6. interruption	
7. mysterious	
8. rival	
9. conjuring	
10. reckless	
11. misery	
12. astonished	
13. wretched	
14. dryly	

Adverbial suffixes

Look at the words in italics in the following sentences. They are called adverbs. These are words that qualify verbs, adjectives, and even other adverbs.

- Leacock looked at the clerks *shyly*.
- He wanted to open a *fairly* large account.
- He left the bank very *fearfully*.

In the first sentence, *shyly* qualifies the verb *looked*. In the second sentence, *fairly* modifies the adjective *large*. And in the third sentence, the adverb *very* qualifies another adverb *fearfully*.

Many adverbs are derived from adjectives and end with the suffix *–ly* for example *shyly, fairly, fearfully,* etc. But some adverbs like *very* are formed without the *–ly* suffix. Here are some examples of such words.

just, too, seldom, almost, also, already, well, quite

Can you add more words to this list?

Words used as adverbs and adjectives

Some adverbs like *fast*, *late,* and *hard* can also function like adjectives. Look at the following sentences and notice how these words are used as both adverbs and adjectives.

1. He walked *fast* because he had missed the *fast* bus.
2. He got to the meeting *late* because he was a *late* riser.
3. He worked *hard,* especially at the *hard* subjects.

It is important to note that the word *fastly* does not occur in English. Although *hardly* and *lately* are used, they have meanings which are unrelated to *hard* and *fast*.

Tendulkar hits the ball *hard*.
He *hardly* ever plays football. (hardly = seldom)

He does not go to the stadium *late* in the night.
Lately he has had a number of accidents.

Look at the use of *hard* and *hardly* in the first pair of sentences and *late* and *lately* in the second pair of sentences. Do you understand the differences in their meaning?

Rewrite the following sentences using the adverbial forms of the words in italics.

Example: When I entered the bank, I was *nervous*.
I entered the bank *nervously*.

1. The accountant said *with certainty* that he would bring the manager.
2. The manager was *cold* when he greeted the customer.
3. The clerks were *happy* to send the customer out.
4. He said he would read the book *at leisure*.
5. Some students are *fortunate* to get jobs as soon as they pass out from college.

Thinking about soft skills

Work in pairs and discuss these questions.

1. What does emotion mean?
2. What does intelligence mean?
3. What do you understand by emotional intelligence?
4. What is emotional quotient? How is it different from intelligence quotient?
5. Why do employers give importance to the emotional intelligence of their employees?

Emotional intelligence skills from the story

The story, 'My Financial Career', tells you about a man who made a mess of a simple bank transaction because he was nervous and afraid of bank officials. If the man's emotional intelligence skills had been better developed, he would have been able to handle the situation in the bank more effectively.

Here is a list of such skills. Read the story and identify which characters either possess or lack these skills.

self-awareness – knowledge of one's own emotions
self-regulation – control over oneself
motivation – goal setting and achievement
empathy – understanding others from their point of view
interaction – working with others and managing conflicts

Activity

1. Answer the following questions which will help you to explore the emotional intelligence skills in the story.

1. Is the narrator aware of the emotions aroused in him when he is at the bank?
2. Does he control his emotions?
3. Does he motivate himself to achieve the objective of opening a bank account?
4. Does he interact with the bank officials in a positive manner?
5. How do the bank officials treat the narrator?
6. What are some positive and negative emotions which are not found in this story?
7. Understanding our emotions and those of others is very useful in developing effective communication skills. Do you agree? Give reasons for your answer.

2. Set a goal for yourself. Write it down here.

My goal: ______________________________
______________________________.

Work with a partner. Discuss each of your goals and see whether they are set according to the SMART principle which is given below.

S – specific
M – measurable
A – achievable
R – realistic/ resource-based
T – time-bound

Now rewrite your goal according to the SMART principle.

My revised goal: ______________________________

3. Work in groups of four and discuss the following situations.

a. Your junior is promoted to a job that you thought the management would give you. Discuss how you feel and how you would interact with the management and your junior after this incident?

b. A colleague has been gossiping and spreading rumours about your character and your ability within and outside the organisation in which you are working. You know that the rumours are baseless. How do you feel about the person who is spreading the rumour? What do you think you can do in this situation?

Proverbs on emotional intelligence

1. **Read the following proverbs from various countries which emphasise the importance of emotional intelligence. Can you add a few more proverbs from your mother tongue or any other language? Which proverb do you like the most? Why? Share your views with the class.**

   a. Be civil to all; serviceable to many; familiar with few; friend to one; enemy to none.
   b. Do unto others as you would wish to be done unto you.
   c. Faults are thick when love is thin.
   d. People who live in glass houses should not throw stones.
   e. If you know what hurts yourself, you know what hurts others.
   f. A soft answer turns away anger.
   g. Hate destroys the one who hates more than the one who is hated.
   h. Anger is a bad adviser.
   i. Where there is a will there is a way.
   j. Good people think about the feelings of their animals.

2. **Choose the proverb which best summarises the article and explain your choice to the class.**

3. **The proverbs in the previous exercise emphasise the importance of emotional intelligence. Write a paragraph of 150 words on the importance of self-awareness and how it helps us in our relationships with ourselves, our family and our colleagues. You may give examples from everyday life or from spiritual and philosophical traditions around the world.**

Soft skills at the workplace

Discuss these questions in groups of four or five and share your answers with the class. Each group can choose one topic.

1. Hurting a customer, means hurting your business and your career.
2. How will you deal with difficult customers or clients?

Real life experience

You may have encountered people like the narrator in a shop or other commercial establishment. In about 100 words, write about the troublesome behaviour of one such person and how it could affect the clientele of the establishment.

Self-assessment

Read the following 'yes' or 'no' questions carefully. If your answer is YES, write 1 in the box. If your answer is NO, write 0 in the box.

	Questions	1 or 0
1.	Do you observe your emotions and those of others?	
2.	Do you differentiate between one emotion and another?	
3.	Do you gain information, knowledge, and wisdom from your emotions?	
4.	Do you guide your thoughts and actions according to the information you have gained?	
5.	Do you work on your emotions to achieve emotional, intellectual, and spiritual growth?	
6.	Do you understand your motivations and actions?	
7.	Do you understand the motivations and actions of others?	
8.	Do you find out about how great leaders achieve success by understanding themselves and the world?	
9.	Do you motivate yourself?	
10.	Do you set goals for yourself?	
11.	Do you have self-control?	
12.	Do you appreciate differences in points of view, outlook, social customs and cultures?	
13.	Do you have the ability to solve emotional problems?	
14.	Do you see the relationship between emotions, thoughts, actions and behaviour?	
15.	Do you recognize and take responsibility for your emotions?	
16.	Do you transform your negative emotions into opportunities for learning and growth?	
17.	Do you help others change their negative emotions into positive ones?	
18.	Do you help others identify their emotions for their own benefit?	

19. Do you fulfill your emotional needs?
20. Do you feel good about yourself?
21. Do you have a sense of harmony and peace within yourself?

If your score is between 15–21, you have excellent emotional intelligence skills. If your score is less than 15, you have to improve your emotional intelligence skills.

Further reading

Here are a few more writings by Stephen Leacock. Read them and if possible, discuss them in the class.

1. The Man in Asbestos: An Allegory of the Future
2. Borrowing a Match
3. The Awful Fate of Melpomenus Jones
4. The Conjuror's Revenge
5. The Arrested Philanthropy of Mr. Tomlinson

4. Assertive Skills

Leading up to the story

Discuss these questions in groups of four or five. The group leader may then present the answers to the class.

1. What is the name given to a person who rings bells in churches?
2. Why does everyone want to have a secure job?
3. When job security is under threat what do people do?
4. When do drastic changes appear in an organisation?
5. What happens when employees are unable to update their skills?

The verger

Read the story by Somerset Maugham. Then answer the questions that follow.

There had been a christening that afternoon at St. Peter's, Neville Square, and Albert Edward Foreman still wore his verger's gown. He kept his new one, its folds as full and stiff though it were made not of alpaca but of perennial bronze, for funerals and weddings (St. Peter's, Neville Square, was a church much favored by the fashionable for these ceremonies) and now he wore only his second-best. He wore it with complacence for it was the dignified symbol of his office, and without it (when he took it off to go home) he had the disconcerting sensation of being somewhat insufficiently clad. He took pains with it; he pressed it and ironed it himself. During the sixteen years he had been verger of this church he had had a succession of such gowns, but he had never been able to throw them away when they were worn out and the complete series, neatly wrapped up in brown paper, lay in the bottom drawers of the wardrobe in his bedroom.

The verger busied himself quietly, replacing the painted wooden cover on the marble font, taking away a chair that had been brought for an infirm old lady, and waited for the vicar to have finished in the vestry so that he could tidy up in there and go home. Presently he saw him walk across the chancel, genuflect in front of the high altar and come down the aisle; but he still wore his cassock.

'What's he 'anging about for?' the verger said to himself 'Don't 'e know I want my tea?'

The vicar had been but recently appointed, a red-faced energetic man in the early forties, and Albert Edward still regretted his predecessor, a clergyman of the old school who preached leisurely sermons in a silvery voice and dined out a great deal with his more aristocratic parishioners. He liked things in church to be just so, but he never fussed; he was not like this new man who wanted to have his finger in every pie. But Albert Edward was tolerant. St. Peter's was in a very good neighbourhood and the parishioners were a very nice class of people. The new vicar had come from the East End and he couldn't be expected to fall in all at once with the discreet ways of his fashionable congregation.

'All this 'ustle,' said Albert Edward. 'But give 'im time, he'll learn.'

When the vicar had walked down the aisle so far that he could address the verger without raising his voice more than was becoming in a place of worship he stopped.

'Foreman, will you come into the vestry for a minute. I have something to say to you.'

'Very good, sir.'

The vicar waited for him to come up and they walked up the church together.

'A very nice christening, I thought sir. Funny 'ow the baby stopped cryin' the moment you took him.'

'I've noticed they very often do,' said the vicar, with a little smile. 'After all I've had a good deal of practice with them.'

It was a source of subdued pride to him that he could nearly always quiet a whimpering infant by the manner in which he held it and he was not unconscious of the amused admiration with which mothers and nurses watched him settle the baby in the crook of his surpliced arm. The verger knew that it pleased him to be complimented on his talent.

The vicar preceded Albert Edward into the vestry. Albert Edward was a trifle surprised to find the two churchwardens there. He had not seen them come in. They gave him pleasant nods.

'Good afternoon, my lord. Good afternoon, sir,' he said to one after the other.

They were elderly men, both of them and they had been churchwardens almost as long as Albert Edward had been verger. They were sitting now at a handsome refectory table that the old vicar had brought many years before from Italy and the vicar sat down in the vacant chair between them. Albert Edward faced them, the table between him and them and wondered with slight uneasiness what the matter was. He remembered still the occasion on which the organist had got in trouble and the bother they had all had to hush things up. In a church like St. Peter's, Neville Square, they couldn't afford scandal. On the vicar's red face was a look of resolute benignity but the others bore an expression that was slightly troubled.

'He's been naggin' them he 'as,' said the verger to himself. 'He's jockeyed them into doin' something, but they don't like it. That's what it is, you mark my words.'

But his thoughts did not appear on Albert Edward's clean cut and distinguished features. He stood in a respectful but not obsequious attitude. He had been in service before he was appointed to his ecclesiastical office, but only in very good houses, and his deportment was irreproachable. Starting as a page-boy in the household of a merchant-prince he had risen by due degrees from the position of fourth to first footman, for a year he had been single-handed butler to a widowed peeress and, till the vacancy occurred at St. Peter's, butler with two men under him in the house of a retired ambassador. He was tall, spare, grave and dignified. He looked, if not like a duke, at least like an actor of the old school who specialized in dukes' parts. He had tact, firmness and self-assurance. His character was unimpeachable. The vicar began briskly.

'Foreman, we've got something rather unpleasant to say to you. You've been here a great many years and I think his lordship and the general agree with me that you've fulfilled the duties of your office to the satisfaction of everybody concerned.'

The two churchwardens nodded.

'But a most extraordinary circumstance came to my knowledge the other day and I felt it my duty to impart it to the churchwardens. I discovered to my astonishment that you could neither read nor write.'

The verger's face betrayed no sign of embarrassment.

'The last vicar knew that, sir,' he replied. 'He said it didn't make no difference. He always said there was a great deal too much education in the world for 'is taste.'

'It's the most amazing thing I ever heard,' cried the general. 'Do you mean to say that you've been verger of this church for sixteen years and never learned to read or write?'

'I went into service when I was twelve sir. The cook in the first place tried to teach me once, but I didn't seem to 'ave the knack for it, and then what with one thing and another I never seemed to 'ave the time. I've never really found the want of it. I think a lot of these young fellows waste a rare lot of time readin' when they might be doin' something useful.'

'But don't you want to know the news?' said the other churchwarden. 'Don't you ever want to write a letter?'

'No, me lord, I seem to manage very well without. And of late years now they've all these pictures in the papers I get to know what's goin' on pretty well. Me wife's quite a scholar and if I want to write a letter she writes it for me. It's not as if I was a bettin' man.'

The two churchwardens gave the vicar a troubled glance and then looked down at the table.

'Well, Foreman, I've talked the matter over with these gentlemen and they quite agree with me that the situation is impossible. At a church like St. Peter's Neville Square, we cannot have a verger who can neither read nor write.'

Albert Edward's thin, sallow face reddened and he moved uneasily on his feet, but he made no reply.

'Understand me, Foreman, I have no complaint to make against you. You do your work quite satisfactorily; I have the highest opinion both of your character and of your capacity; but we haven't the right to take the risk of some accident that might happen owing to your lamentable ignorance. It's a matter of prudence as well as of principle.'

'But couldn't you learn, Foreman?' asked the general.

'No, sir, I'm afraid I couldn't, not now. You see, I'm not as young as I was and if I couldn't seem able to get the letters in me 'ead when I was a nipper I don't think there's much chance of it now.'

'We don't want to be harsh with you, Foreman,' said the vicar. 'But the churchwardens and I have quite made up our minds. We'll give you three months and if at the end of that time you cannot read and write I'm afraid you'll have to go.'

Albert Edward had never liked the new vicar. He'd said from the beginning that they'd made a mistake when they gave him St. Peter's. He wasn't the type of man they wanted with a classy congregation like that. And now he straightened himself a little. He knew his value and he wasn't going to allow himself to be put upon.

'I'm very sorry sir, I'm afraid it's no good. I'm too old a dog to learn new tricks. I've lived a good many years without knowin' 'ow to read and write, and without wishin' to praise myself, self-praise is no recommendation, I don't mind sayin' I've done my duty in that state of life in which it 'as pleased a merciful providence to place me, and if I could learn now I don't know as I'd want to.'

'In that case, Foreman, I'm afraid you must go.'

'Yes sir, I quite understand. I shall be 'appy to 'and in my resignation as soon as you've found somebody to take my place.'

But when Albert Edward with his usual politeness had closed the church door behind the vicar and the two churchwardens he could not sustain the air of unruffled dignity with which he had borne the blow inflicted upon him and his lips quivered. He walked slowly back to the vestry and hung up on its proper peg his verger's gown. He sighed as he thought of all the grand funerals and smart weddings it had seen. He tidied everything up, put on his coat, and hat in hand walked down the aisle. He locked the church door behind him. He strolled across the square, but deep in his sad thoughts he did not take the street that led him home, where a nice strong cup of tea awaited; he took the wrong turning. He walked slowly along. His heart was heavy. He did not know what he should do with himself. He did not fancy the notion of going back to domestic service; after being his own master for so many years, for the vicar and churchwardens could say what they liked, it was he that had run St. Peter's, Neville Square, he could scarcely demean himself by accepting a situation. He had saved a tidy sum, but not enough to live on without doing something, and life seemed to cost more every year. He had never thought to be troubled with such questions. The vergers of St. Peter's, like the popes of Rome, were there for life. He had often thought of the pleasant reference the vicar would make in his sermon at evensong the first Sunday after his death to the long and faithful service, and the exemplary character of their late verger, Albert Edward Foreman. He sighed deeply. Albert Edward was a non-smoker and a total abstainer, but with a certain latitude; that is to say he liked a glass of beer with his dinner and when he was tired he enjoyed a cigarette. It occurred to him now that one would comfort him and since he did not carry them he looked about him for a shop where he could buy a packet of Gold Flakes. He did not at once see one and walked on a little. It was a long street with all sorts of shops in it, but there was not a single one where you could buy cigarettes.

'That's strange,' said Albert Edward.

To make sure he walked right up the street again. No, there was no doubt about it. He stopped and looked reflectively up and down.

'I can't be the only man as walks along this street and wants a fag,' he said. 'I shouldn't wonder but what a fellow might do very well with a little shop here. Tobacco and sweets, you know.'

He gave a sudden start.

'That's an idea,' he said. 'Strange 'ow things come to you when you least expect it.'

He turned, walked home, and had his tea.

'You're very silent this afternoon, Albert,' his wife remarked.

'I'm thinkin',' he said.

He considered the matter from every point of view and next day he went along the street and by good luck found a little shop to let that looked as though it would exactly suit him. Twenty-four hours later he had taken it and when a month after that he left St. Peter's, Neville Square, for ever, Albert Edward Foreman set up in business as a tobacconist and newsagent. His wife said it was a dreadful come-down after being verger of St. Peter's, but he answered that you had to move with the times, the church wasn't what it was, and 'enceforward he was going to render unto Caesar what was Caesar's. Albert Edward did very well. He did so well that in a year or so it struck him that he might take a second shop and put a manager in. He looked for another long street that hadn't got a tobacconist in it and when he found it and a shop to let, took it and stocked it. This was a success too. Then it occurred to him that if he could run two he could run half a dozen, so he began walking about London, and whenever he found a long street that had no tobacconist and a shop to let he took it. In the course of ten years he had acquired no less than ten shops and he was making money hand over fist. He went round to all of them himself every Monday, collected the week's takings and took them to the bank.

One morning when he was there paying in a bundle of notes and a heavy bag of silver the cashier told him that the manager would like to see him. He was shown into an office and the manager shook hands with him.

'Mr. Foreman, I wanted to have a talk to you about the money you've got on deposit with us. D'you know exactly how much it is?'

'Not within a pound or two, sir; but I've got a pretty rough idea.'

'Apart from what you paid in this morning it's a little over thirty thousand pounds. That's a very large sum to have on deposit and I should have thought you'd do better to invest it.'

'I wouldn't want to take no risk, sir. I know it's safe in the bank.'

'You needn't have the least anxiety. We'll make you out a list of absolutely gilt-edged securities. They'll bring you in a better rate of interest than we can possibly afford to give you.'

A troubled look settled on Mr. Foreman's distinguished face. 'I've never 'ad anything to do with stocks and shares and I'd 'ave to leave it all in your 'ands,' he said.

The manager smiled. 'We'll do everything. All you'll have to do next time you come in is just to sign the transfers.'

'I could do that all right,' said Albert uncertainly. 'But 'ow should I know what I was signin'?'

'I suppose you can read,' said the manager a trifle sharply.

Mr. Foreman gave him a disarming smile.

'Well, sir, that's just it. I can't. I know it sounds funny-like but there it is, I can't read or write, only me name, an' I only learnt to do that when I went into business.'

The manager was so surprised that he jumped up from his chair. 'That's the most extraordinary thing I ever heard.'

'You see it's like this, sir, I never 'ad the opportunity until it was too late and then some'ow I wouldn't. I got obstinate-like.'

The manager stared at him as though he were a prehistoric monster. 'And do you mean to say that you've built up this important business and amassed a fortune of thirty thousand pounds without being able to read or write? Good God, man, what would you be now if you had been able to?'

'I can tell you that sir,' said Mr. Foreman, a little smile on his still aristocratic features. 'I'd be verger of St. Peter's, Neville Square.'

Somerset Maugham

Understanding the story

Answer the following questions. Later you may discuss your answers in the class.

1. Who is Albert Edward?
2. How long has he been working at his job?
3. What is his attitude to the new vicar?

4. What problem does Albert face in his career?
5. How does he face the critical situation that he no longer has a job?
6. How does he set up a new business and prosper in it?
7. Why does the bank manager want to speak to Albert Edward?
8. What does the bank manager come to know about Albert Edward?
9. Why is the bank manager surprised?
10. What is your opinion about the last sentence of the story?

Understanding people and places

In what locations can the characters in the story be found? Against each person, write the places in which the action of the story locates them. For example, the vicar is in the vestry. Some people may be located in more than one place.

People	Places
1.	
2.	
3.	
4.	
5.	

Vocabulary development

Meanings in context

Look up a dictionary and find the meanings of the words and phrases below, as they are used in the context of the story

Words and phrases	Meanings
1. alpaca	
2. complacence	
3. disconcerting	
4. chancel	
5. genuflect	
6. cassock	
7. discreet	
8. congregation	
9. surpliced	
10. refectory	

11. jockeyed
12. obsequious
13. ecclesiastical
14. deportment
15. irreproachable
16. unimpeachable
17. sallow
18. lamentable
19. prudence
20. latitude

Verbs and verb suffixes

Regular and irregular verbs

Look at these words. They belong to a group of words called verbs, which indicate doing or action.

christen, wore, kept, took, pressed, disconcert, ironed, lay, busied, replaced, waited, took, saw, hang, said, know, want, appointed, regretted, preached, dined, liked, guessed

There are two types of verbs—regular and irregular verbs.

Regular verbs have some regularity and predictability in the formation of the past and past participle forms. For example: *walk – walked – walked*, *press – pressed – pressed, iron – ironed – ironed, wait – waited – waited*. These verbs usually end in an *-ed* suffix.

Irregular verbs however, have variations in the past and past participle forms. For example: *take – took – taken, wear – wore – worn, keep – kept – kept.*

Irregular verbs are often difficult for learners of English. The only solution is to learn them and use them often in oral and written communication.

Identify ten regular and ten irregular verbs from the story and complete the table. Give the past and past participle forms of the irregular verbs. The first one has been done for you.

	Regular verbs			Irregular verbs		
	Base form	Past form	Past participle form	Base form	Past form	Past participle form
1.	fold	folded	folded	keep	kept	kept
2.						
3.						
4.						

5.
6.
7.
8.
9.
10.

VERB SUFFIXES

Verbs can be made from nouns and adjectives with the help of a few suffixes like -*ise*, -*fy*, -*ate*, and -*en*. For example, *specialise, redden, educate* and *dignify* are verbs derived from *special, red, education,* and *dignity*.

Make verbs from the following words using appropriate suffixes.

	words	verbs		words	verbs
1.	strength		11.	pure	
2.	character		12.	isolation	
3.	exemplary		13.	deep	
4.	hesitation		14.	general	
5.	notification		15.	sweet	
6.	separation		16.	energetic	
7.	sharp		17.	hard	
8.	picture		18.	symbol	
9.	beauty		19.	specific	
10.	demonstration		20.	magnificent	

WORDS USED AS VERBS AND NOUNS

Look at the words in italics in the following sentences.

- Albert is the *master* of his own destiny. He *mastered* the art of taking life in his own hands and changing it for the better
- The new vicar asked Albert a disturbing *question*. But Albert did not *question* the authority of his employer.

In these sentences, *master* and *question* have been used as both verbs and nouns.

Here are some words from the passage. Make sentences of your own using each word as a verb and a noun.

1. service
2. practice
3. walk
4. bank
5. pay
6. bundle

7. need	14. second
8. comfort	15. interest
9. wonder	16. stock
10. point	17. share
11. view	18. smile
12. answer	19. transfer
13. cost	20. trouble

Thinking about soft skills

Work in pairs and discuss these questions.

1. What is assertiveness?
2. How is assertiveness different from aggression?
3. What are the characteristics of an assertive person?
4. Why do employers prefer assertive candidates?

Assertive skills from the story

Assertiveness means the ability to express opinions or desires strongly and with confidence, so that people take notice. Assertive people understand their rights and responsibilities and stand up for them. They are not afraid to say 'no,' if the situation demands it. They are not shy, or hesitant to ask for clarification from others. They ask for help when it is needed. Their body language shows confidence and belief in themselves.

In contrast to assertive behaviour, are two undesirable types of behaviour. These are submissiveness and aggression. While submissiveness refers to agreeing to everything at the cost of pain to oneself, aggression refers to achieving one's goals unmindful of how others suffer. Both behaviours lead to problems in human relationships.

In the story 'The Verger,' the foreman states his position clearly and confidently. He says that he cannot learn to read and write at his age. He knows that he has to give up his job, yet he does not behave in a way that will allow him to keep the job but lose his self-respect. To tide over his crisis, he establishes a petty shop and becomes a big businessman. In the end he is also willing to risk investing his money in shares and stocks. Thus he displays the assertive skills required for success in life.

Here is a list of skills from the story. Read the story and find out when Albert Edward displayed each of these skills.

1. Being able to say 'no'
2. Complimenting others when they do a good job

3. Asking for time to think and decide
4. Visualising something and making it happen
5. Reliving a successful event in the past

Activity

There are many occasions in your personal and professional life when you have to be assertive. Here are some situations for you to role play.

1. A twenty-twenty cricket match is going to be held in your town a few days before your semester examination. Some of your friends plan to watch the game instead of preparing for the examination. You have to refuse to join them politely but firmly. However, you must not lose their good will. You will need at least three students for this role play.
2. Your classmate has come back from the US after making a presentation in a technical seminar. You feel envious, yet you have to congratulate him. How do you do it?
3. Recall a moment in your life when you achieved some success or victory. You must think aloud and reflect on your experiences in front of the class.
4. Your teacher tells you to submit your assignment tomorrow. You have to politely request your teacher to allow you to submit the assignment two days later.

Proverbs on assertive skills

1. **Read the following proverbs from various countries about the importance of assertiveness. Can you add a few more proverbs from your mother tongue or any other language? Which proverb do you like the most? Why? Share your views with the class.**
   a. He who asks is a fool for five minutes but he who does not ask remains a fool forever.
   b. Kill your enemies with your kindness.
   c. If you cannot make a person think as you do, make a person do as you think.
   d. Seek till you find and you will not lose labour.
   e. We do not walk on our legs, but on our will.
   f. A person who will not flee will make his foe flee.
   g. He who does not cry does not get fed.
   h. Put your feet down where you mean to stand.
   i. Speak the truth in love.
   j. Come and let us reason together.
2. **You need strength of mind and body to be true to yourself and behave in accordance with your goals and preferences without hurting others around you. These proverbs**

focus on understanding, determination, self-confidence and persistence which are necessary for you to achieve your goal and also help others to achieve theirs.

Write a paragraph of 150 words on how assertive skills can benefit your personal and professional development.

Soft skills at the workplace

Discuss these questions in groups of four or five and share your answers with the class. Each group can choose one topic.

1. What are the reasons for the mismatch between education and employment?
2. What personal qualities can help you achieve assertive behaviour?
3. Many great people did not have the advantage of a good education. Benjamin Franklin, Thomas Alva Edison, Henry Ford, Srinivasa Ramanujan, and Dhirubhai Ambani are well known examples. What qualities and characteristics helped these people achieve greatness in their chosen fields?

Real life experience

You may know about people who were forced to quit their jobs. In 150 words write about one person and how he or she coped with the situation. Try to think of someone who later became successful.

Self-assessment

Read the following 'yes' or 'no' questions carefully. If your answer is YES, write 1. If your answer is NO, write 0.

	Questions	1 or 0
1.	Do you stand up and speak up for yourself?	
2.	Do you speak directly but politely?	
3.	Do you express your ideas effectively?	
4.	Do you convey your wishes and concerns clearly?	
5.	Do you offer excuses or apologies appropriately?	
6.	Do you make other people feel comfortable?	
7.	Do you tackle demanding and commanding people tactfully?	
8.	Do you keep your self-respect in all situations?	
9.	Do you exude warmth in your interactions?	
10.	Do you elicit the expected response in your listener?	

11. Do you maintain goodwill even with irritating and annoying people?
12. Do you make sure that other people do not lose face?
13. Do you empathise with people?
14. Do you say 'no' to others gracefully?
15. Do you stop trying to please people beyond a point?
16. Do you have the courage to work with people you do not like?
17. Do you handle criticism graciously?
18. Do you participate in group discussions freely?
19. Do you manage your feelings of anger, fear and hatred well?
20. Do you use fair and unbiased language in your communication?
21. Do you follow the principle of 'live and let live'?

If your score is between 15-21, you have excellent assertive skills. If your score is less than 15, you have to improve your assertive skills.

Further reading

Here are a few more stories by Somerset Maugham. Read them and, if possible, discuss them in the class.

1. The Ant and the Grasshopper
2. Mr. Know-It-All
3. The Luncheon
4. A Friend in Need
5. In a Strange Land

5. Learning Skills

Leading up to the story

Discuss these questions in groups of four or five. The group leader may then present the answers to the class.

1. In the past, it was essential for kings to possess certain skills. What were these skills and how did they acquire them?
2. What role did *rishis* play in the lives of kings and princes in India?
3. There are many stories about *rishis* and their wisdom in Indian mythology. Which legendary *rishi* stands out in your mind? Why?

Three questions

Read the story by Leo Tolstoy. Then answer the questions that follow.

It once occurred to a certain king, that if he always knew the right time to begin everything; if he knew who were the right people to listen to, and whom to avoid; and, above all, if he always knew what was the most important thing to do, he would never fail in anything he might undertake.

And this thought having occurred to him, he had it proclaimed throughout his kingdom that he would give a great reward to any one who would teach him what was the right time for every action, and who were the most necessary people, and how he might know what was the most important thing to do.

And learned men came to the King, but they all answered his questions differently.

In reply to the first question, some said that to know the right time for every action, one must draw up in advance, a table of days, months and years, and must live strictly according to it. Only thus, said they, could everything be done at its proper time. Others declared that it was impossible to decide beforehand the right time for every action; but that, not letting oneself be absorbed in idle pastimes, one should always attend to all that was going on, and then do what was most needful. Others, again, said that however attentive the King might be to what was going on, it was impossible for one man to decide correctly the right time for every action, but that he should have a Council of wise men, who would help him to fix the proper time for everything.

But then again others said there were some things which could not wait to be laid before a Council, but about which one had at once to decide whether to undertake them or not. But in order to decide that, one must know beforehand what was going to happen. It is only magicians who know that; and, therefore, in order to know the right time for every action, one must consult magicians.

Equally various were the answers to the second question. Some said, the people the King most needed were his councilors; others, the priests; others, the doctors; while some said the warriors were the most necessary.

To the third question, as to what was the most important occupation: some replied that the most important thing in the world was science. Others said it was skill in warfare; and others, again, that it was religious worship.

All the answers being different, the King agreed with none of them, and gave the reward to none. But still wishing to find the right answers to his questions, he decided to consult a hermit, widely renowned for his wisdom.

The hermit lived in a wood which he never quitted, and he received none but common folk. So the King put on simple clothes, and before reaching the hermit's cell dismounted from his horse, and, leaving his body-guard behind, went on alone.

When the King approached, the hermit was digging the ground in front of his hut. Seeing the King, he greeted him and went on digging. The hermit was frail and weak, and each time he stuck his spade into the ground and turned a little earth, he breathed heavily.

The King went up to him and said: 'I have come to you, wise hermit, to ask you to answer three questions: How can I learn to do the right thing at the right time? Who are the people I most need, and to whom should I, therefore, pay more attention than to the rest? And, what affairs are the most important, and need my first attention?'

The hermit listened to the King, but answered nothing. He just spat on his hand and recommenced digging.

'You are tired,' said the King, 'let me take the spade and work awhile for you.'

'Thanks!' said the hermit, and, giving the spade to the King, he sat down on the ground.

When he had dug two beds, the King stopped and repeated his questions. The hermit again gave no answer, but rose, stretched out his hand for the spade, and said:

'Now rest awhile—and let me work a bit.'

But the King did not give him the spade, and continued to dig. One hour passed, and another. The sun began to sink behind the trees, and the King at last stuck the spade into the ground, and said:

'I came to you, wise man, for an answer to my questions. If you can give me none, tell me so, and I will return home.'

'Here comes someone running,' said the hermit, 'let us see who it is.'

The King turned round, and saw a bearded man come running out of the wood. The man held his hands pressed against his stomach, and blood was flowing from under them. When he reached the King, he fell fainting on the ground moaning feebly. The King and the hermit unfastened the man's clothing. There was a large wound in his stomach. The King washed it as best he could, and bandaged it with his handkerchief and with a towel the hermit had. But the blood would not stop flowing, and the King again and again removed the bandage soaked with warm blood, and washed and rebandaged the wound. When at last the blood ceased flowing, the man revived and asked for something to drink. The King brought fresh water and gave it to him. Meanwhile the sun had set, and it had become cool. So the King, with the hermit's help, carried the wounded man into the hut and laid him on the bed. Lying on the bed the man closed his eyes and was quiet; but the King was so tired with his walk and with the work he had done, that he crouched down on the threshold, and also fell asleep—so soundly that he slept all through the short summer night. When he awoke in the morning, it was long before he could remember where he was, or who was the strange bearded man lying on the bed and gazing intently at him with shining eyes.

'Forgive me!' said the bearded man in a weak voice, when he saw that the King was awake and was looking at him.

'I do not know you, and have nothing to forgive you for,' said the King.

'You do not know me, but I know you. I am that enemy of yours who swore to revenge himself on you, because you executed his brother and seized his property. I knew you had gone alone to see the hermit, and I resolved to kill you on your way back. But the day passed and you did not return. So I came out from my ambush to find you, and I came upon your bodyguard, and they recognized me, and wounded me. I escaped from them, but should have bled to death had you not dressed my wound. I wished to kill you, and you have saved my life. Now, if I live, and if you wish it, I will serve you as your most faithful slave, and will bid my sons do the same. Forgive me!'

The King was very glad to have made peace with his enemy so easily, and to have gained him for a friend, and he not only forgave him, but said he would send his servants and his own physician to attend him, and promised to restore his property.

Having taken leave of the wounded man, the King went out into the porch and looked around for the hermit. Before going away he wished once more to beg an answer to the questions he had put. The hermit was outside, on his knees, sowing seeds in the beds that had been dug the day before.

The King approached him, and said:

'For the last time, I pray you to answer my questions, wise man.'

'You have already been answered!' said the hermit, still crouching on his thin legs, and looking up at the King, who stood before him.

'How answered? What do you mean?' asked the King.

'Do you not see,' replied the hermit. 'If you had not pitied my weakness yesterday, and had not dug those beds for me, but had gone your way, that man would have attacked you, and you would have repented of not having stayed with me. So the most important time was when you were digging the beds; and I was the most important man; and to do me good was your most important business. Afterwards when that man ran to us, the most important time was when you were attending to him, for if you had not bound up his wounds he would have died without having made peace with you. So he was the most important man, and what you did for him was your most important business. Remember then: there is only one time that is important—Now! It is the most important time because it is the only time when we have any power. The most necessary man is he with whom you are, for no man knows whether he will ever have dealings with any one else: and the most important affair is, to do him good, because for that purpose alone was man sent into this life!'

Leo Tolstoy

Understanding the story

Answer the following questions. Later you may discuss your answers in the class.

1. What does the king want to know?
2. Why did the king want this knowledge?
3. Why is he dissatisfied with the answers that people gave him?
4. Who does he turn to for an answer?
5. Why is the king willing to dig the ground for the learned man?
6. Why does the king repeat his question to the learned man several times?
7. What happens to prevent the king from returning home?
8. Why does the king forgive his enemy and restore his property?
9. How does the learned man explain the incident of the wounded man?
10. What lesson does the king learn from the hermit?

Understanding people

There are five characters in this story. What is the nature of their relationships with other people? What motivates them to help or hinder others by being friendly or inimical? Write your observations in the table below.

People	Relationships with others
1. The king and the hermit	
2. The learned men and the king	
3. The hermit and the king	
4. The enemy and the soldiers	
5. The soldiers and the king	

Vocabulary development

Meanings in context

Look up a dictionary and find the meanings of the words and phrases below, as they are used in the context of the story.

	Words and phrases	Meanings
1.	proclaimed	
2.	draw up	
3.	hermit	
4.	renowned	
5.	cell	
6.	dismounted	
7.	frail	
8.	recommenced	
9.	feebly	
10.	ceased	
11.	revived	
12.	crouched	
13.	threshold	
14.	ambush	
15.	repented	

Pronouns

So far you have learned the most important building blocks of English vocabulary — nouns, adjectives, adverbs, and verbs. Hereafter you will learn more about another set of vocabulary whose number is limited but whose function is very significant in making and conveying meaning. We shall start with pronouns — words which can be used instead of nouns. Pronouns have an important function in communication. They refer back to or replace a noun and thus add to the well-knit structure of a passage.

The seven pronouns in English are: I, we, you, he, she, it, and they.

I — first person singular

we — first person plural

you — second person singular and plural

he — third person singular masculine

she — third person singular feminine

it —third person singular neutral

they — third person plural

These personal pronouns have different forms, depending upon their position in a sentence and relation to the nouns they stand for. For example, 'I' has these forms: *me, my, mine*. Look at these examples.

- *I* have a book.
- The teacher gave it to *me*.
- It is *my* favorite book.
- The book is *mine* forever

1. Here is a list of personal pronouns. Complete the table with the different forms of these pronouns. Then make sentences to illustrate how they are used.

I	me	my	mine
We			
You			
He			
She			
It			
They			

2. Read the following passages and underline the pronouns. Then identify the nouns to which the pronouns refer.

a. When the King approached, the hermit was digging the ground in front of his hut. Seeing the King, he greeted him and went on digging. The hermit was frail and weak, and each time he stuck his spade into the ground and turned a little earth, he breathed heavily.

b. The King turned round, and saw a bearded man come running out of the wood. The man held his hands pressed against his stomach, and blood was flowing from under them. When he reached the King, he fell fainting on the ground moaning feebly. The King and the hermit unfastened the man's clothing. There was a large wound in his stomach. The King washed it as best he could, and bandaged it with his handkerchief and with a towel the hermit had.

3. Rewrite the following passage with the correct pronouns.

Radha is an efficient lady. They go to office on time. She does not even go to the canteen for his lunch. Naturally, he finishes my work every day. Their manager, Mr. Santhosh Gupta, is very pleased with his performance. He plans to recommend a rise in pay for them from next month.

Prefixes

Look at the following words.

impossible, dismounted, unfastened

These words begin with the prefixes *im–*, *dis–*, and *un–*. These are negative prefixes and are added to words to form their opposite. Thus, *im*+ *possible* = *impossible*.

1. Here is a list of negative prefixes with examples of words that can be made with each of them. Add two more words for each prefix.

	Prefixes	Examples	Your words
1.	a-	amoral	
2.	anti-	anti-social	
3.	contra-	contradictory	
4.	counter-	counter-point	
5.	de-	decentralize	
6.	dis-	discontinue	
7.	il-	illiterate	
8.	im-	immovable	
9.	in-	infinite	
10.	ir-	irregular	
11.	mal-	malpractice	
12.	mis-	misunderstand	
13.	non-	non-cooperation	
14.	sub-	sub-standard	
15.	un-	unnecessary	
16.	under-	underestimate	

2. Write the opposites of the following words using suitable prefixes.

	Words	Opposites		Words	Opposites
1.	certain		5.	skilled	
2.	important		6.	agreed	
3.	action		7.	common	
4.	proper		8.	learn	

9. attentive
10. correctly
11. wise
12. equally
13. known
14. religious
15. quiet
16. done
17. faithful
18. easy
19. continue
20. recognise

Thinking about soft skills

Work in pairs and discuss these questions.

1. Why is it important to update one's knowledge and skills?
2. What are the different sources you can use to acquire knowledge?
3. What motivates some people to study and learn even when there is no apparent need to do so?

Learning skills from the story

In the story the king wants the answers to three important questions so that he can rule his country effectively. The desire to learn is so great that even though he is a king he is willing to do manual work for the hermit.

He sets himself a learning goal and does not stop till he achieves his objective. He starts to learn because he has already assessed the areas in which he needs to develop. If he felt that he knew everything, he would never begin the process of learning. He identifies the people who can teach him and when he is not satisfied he looks further till he finds the learned man. He learns to forgive the man who comes to kill him and in the process, strengthens his friendship with the man.

Activity

Discuss this question in groups.

A person who has the ability to learn has some of the following traits. Do you think the king has any of these traits? Give examples from the story to support your answer.

1. Humility
2. An awareness of one's limitations
3. Generosity
4. A willingness to risk failure
5. Curiosity

Proverbs on learning skills

1. **Read the following proverbs from various countries about the importance of learning. Can you add a few more proverbs from your mother tongue or any other language? Which proverb do you like the most? Why? Share your views with the class.**

   a. He who is afraid of asking is ashamed of learning.
   b. The gem cannot be polished without friction, nor man perfected without trials.
   c. Only after learning, do you know what you do not know.
   d. You are never too old to learn.
   e. Learning is a treasure that will follow its owner everywhere.
   f. Keep the old, but learn the new.
   g. You will not grow at all if you think you know it all.
   h. If you study to remember you forget; but if you study to understand, you will remember.
   i. Live and learn.
   j. If the child is not learning the way you are teaching, then you must teach in the way the child learns.

2. **Choose the proverb which best summarises the story and explain your choice to the class.**

3. **Use the questions below as a guide to help you write a paragraph on learning in about 150 words.**

   a. What prevents us from learning?
   b. What happens to people who stop learning?
   c. All children have the ability to learn but some fail to learn even those basic skills which are necessary for their survival. Why?
   d. Why are learned people respected everywhere?
   e. How do learned people manage to live well even in difficult circumstances?

Role play

Work in pairs and enact this situation.

Think about something you have wanted to learn but have been prevented from doing so. For example, you may have wanted to learn a computer language, driving, swimming, singing, playing a musical instrument, dancing, or pursue a course of study. Imagine that you get an opportunity to fulfill your dreams. Meet the instructor and ask questions regarding your course.

Soft skills in the workplace

Discuss these questions in groups of four or five and share your answers with the class. Each group can choose one topic.

1. You have been working in a company for many years and your employees are satisfied with your work. Suddenly one day you are asked to upgrade your skills. What will you do to improve your skills?
2. What are the different ways by which you can acquire recognised degrees and diplomas?
3. What are the informal ways of learning by which you can develop your abilities and empower yourself?
4. What opportunities are given to employees to improve their skills and abilities? Give specific examples.

Self-assessment

Read the following 'yes' or 'no' questions carefully. If your answer is YES, write 1. If your answer is NO, write 0.

	Questions	1 or 0
1.	Do you have the willingness to learn?	
2.	Do you have the willingness to learn continuously?	
3.	Do you assess your personal strengths and weaknesses?	
4.	Do you set learning goals for yourself?	
5.	Do you identify and access learning sources and opportunities?	
6.	Do you plan for and achieve your learning goals?	
7.	Do you listen carefully during discussions?	
8.	Do you know when you have learnt enough and can stop researching a topic?	
9.	Do you make notes on the topics you read?	
10.	Do you seek help when needed?	
11.	Do you use diagrams to illustrate your points?	
12.	Do you organise your ideas coherently?	
13.	Do you collect and include relevant information in your writing?	
14.	Do you develop logical conclusions from your study?	
15.	Do you put ideas in your own words?	
16.	Do you have an open mind towards new ideas?	
17.	Do you try out new ideas?	
18.	Do you take time to think about different ideas?	

19. Do you use technology to quicken your learning?
20. Do you read widely in different subject areas?
21. Do you read with understanding?

If your score is between 15–21, you have excellent learning skills. If your score is less than 15, you have to improve your learning skills.

Further reading

Here are a few more stories by Leo Tolstoy. Read them and, if possible, discuss them in the class.

1. Three Hermits
2. Little Girls Wiser Than Men
3. How Much Land Does a Man Need?
4. Too Dear
5. Ilyas

6. Problem-Solving Skills

Leading up to the story

Discuss these questions in groups of four or five. The group leader may then present the answers to the class.

1. What are the different kinds of jewellery shops you are familiar with?
2. Where do the rich and fashionable buy their jewellery?
3. Why are safety measures important for big jewellery shops? What safety measures do they use?

The look-out man

Read the story by Nicolas Bentley. Then answer the questions that follow.

My name is William Morris (no relation to the famous one; my folks came from Salford). I shall be fifty-three this year, married, with one daughter (also married), and I live at Woldingham in Surrey. I am what you call one of the quiet sort, I suppose. My life may not seem very exciting to some people, but that is the way I like to lead it.

I am fond of reading (there is enough excitement for me in books) and I like painting (only water colors as yet) and doing odds and ends about the house. So perhaps there is a bit of the other Morris in me after all; he was fond of doing odd jobs, too.

Although I am such a great reader, I had never thought of writing anything until this great event in my life happened and I felt I had to record it. So I must ask you to grin and bear it if my shortcomings as author appear too obvious.

For more than thirty years I have made a study of detective fiction. But I do not read trash, and Heaven knows, there is enough of that about. Poe and Collins and Gaboriau, and of course, Holmes, and later on Trent and Dr Thorndyke were what shaped my taste for detective stories.

And what I call detective stories are ones that deal with real detection, where the detective is not just a kind of superman but an ordinary one who has nothing but sharp eyes and common sense to rely on.

Consequently I think I have learned to look more closely at my fellow men than most people usually do. But it is not out of curiosity; it is for what it can teach you about human nature in general.

After all, it is the same method as bird watchers use, and it seems to me you can tell as much about a publican as a pelican if you look at him long enough. (Not that I am a frequenter of pubs, because my wife is a total abstainer.)

I seldom go in a bus or train or anywhere without learning something about the people around me that you might easily miss at first glance. I like to study (quite unobtrusively, of course) the details and the state of their clothing, their hands and teeth and hair, and their jewellery (if any), and spectacles and fountain pens and so on, and what they are reading or carrying, and the way they talk and walk.

You cannot make much out of a single fact, of course, but put two facts together and you may have enough to hang a man on.

I expect my deductions are quite often wrong. I seldom have any means of proving them. But at any rate they keep my imagination more lively than doing crosswords, and for the interest I get they are a lot more profitable to me than doing the pools, of that I am sure.

Every day as I come up in the train—I work at Regnier's, the antique jewellers in Knightsbridge—I sit and look. But I have never had to put my powers of observation to the test, except when we had this trouble in the shop.

We have a very fine stock of old jewellery, but naturally we do not display much of this, except in the window which is well protected. We carry also a big range of objets d'art, Faberge and cloisonné articles, small carvings, crystal, jade and so on, and these are what we have on show.

The only assistants are Miss Susskind and I. (The repairs man *works off* the premises.) Mr Regnier only attends special customers and big buyers.

The first thing that I do in the morning is to re-dress the window (we always clear it at night), and on this particular morning I happened to notice a girl looking in the window of the undertaker's opposite; though beyond a couple of urns and a photo of a hearse there cannot have been much to interest a girl, and I remember wondering about this at the time.

The reason I noticed her (I do not usually 'notice' girls; they are all one to me now a days, except as subjects of disinterested speculation) was because of her overcoat. It was a long yellow coat with big brown checks. And she had long yellow hair as well.

She was what you would call distinctly an 'arty' type—no hat and low heels, and I should imagine principles that were not much higher, from the general look of her.

I watched her for a little while, then I was interrupted by a customer. He was one of those gum-chewing Americans, but quite quiet in his looks, except for the pattern on his tie, which looked more like an accident than a design. I should have said he was between thirty-five and forty. He had a very smooth-looking pink face and was rather a big man.

He came straight in and asked to see some rings. I brought out a couple of trays, just to get some idea of the sort of thing he was after. But I could soon see he knew nothing about antique jewellery; nor anything else antique, I imagined, unless it came out of a bottle.

He asked the price of several rings and picked up two or three—it was then I noticed he was completely left-handed—and looked at them. But you could tell he knew nothing whatever about stones or settings. The only thing he seemed to judge them by was the price.

There was one ring, early seventeenth century, diamonds and rubies in a floral motif, and my word, it was a beauty! Mr Regnier was so fond of it he did not really want to *part with* it, so had put a fancy price on it. It was too fancy for this American, anyway. Not that he could tell the finer rings from those not absolutely of the first water.

Finally there were three trays on the counter in front of him, and he still could not *make up* his mind. Then he spotted a fourth tray in the safe, which was open just behind me, and asked if he could see that, too. So I got it out for him. But even before I had laid it on the counter I spotted that the diamond and ruby floral pattern had walked.

I felt quite stunned—and embarrassed. It had never, never happened to me before, not in all my seventeen years, that anything in my charge at the shop had vanished.

I put down the tray and I made a signal to Miss Susskind with my eyebrows. She came over and when she was close enough to bear witness I said to the customer—and I had a hard job to keep my voice steady:

'You have decided on the floral ring, have you, sir? If you will just let me have it, I will find a box for it ...'

I held out my hand. The American said (I remember exactly his words):

'I haven't decided anything. Why, I just want to pick a couple or so for my wife to choose from. Then I'll have her come in later on.'

What I said exactly I do not now recall, except that it was something to gain time so I could collect myself. I am seldom at my best taken unawares.

Miss Susskind (she is no fool) *slipped off* at once to fetch Mr Regnier. I came round from behind the counter and began looking everywhere, so did the customer, and Miss Susskind and Mr Regnier, too, when they came in.

Of course, Mr Regnier was in a state. He is rather an excitable man, but overcomes it as a rule because he places high premium on his dignity. The American did not like it when Mr Regnier began to *warm up* (no *accusations*, of course; that would never do) and for one minute I thought that things looked like getting rather ugly.

Then Miss Susskind (why she of all people should think of it I do not know) suggested that he should look in his turn-ups. Instead, he looked at her, very hard. His face had gone quite red, so it seemed to me, he had left off chewing and his jaw was set like a trap. From his expression he would like to have caught Miss Susskind's leg in it.

But he bent down and felt all round his turn-ups all the same without any result. Then he burst out laughing.

Sense of humour is not my strong point, I realise that, but even I could see that at this moment Miss Susskind on all-fours was legitimate food for a smile.

Then the American said: 'Why, darn't it, I guess you think I've purloined it or something!'

Of course, faced with such a statement Mr Regnier had to demur. He got up off the carpet and asked the customer very politely, to step into the office.

There (he told me afterwards) he put it quite straight to him, while he did not for one moment suspect him of theft, he must, for insurance purposes, satisfy himself that the ring had not accidentally got into any crease or cranny of his clothing.

It appears that the customer was quite good-natured and understanding about it, or seemed to be, and stripped right down for Mr Regnier, even to his socks and shoes. But there was not a trace of the ring anywhere.

Miss Susskind and I went on looking for it meanwhile, not that I was in very high hopes. It had gone so swiftly and suddenly I could not help but feel suspicious.

While we were still looking another customer came in. And who she be but the girl I had seen not ten minutes since, *looking into* the undertaker's window. There was no reason really why I should have felt surprise, but I did feel it was a coincidence.

Close-to there were several little tell-tale things, her hair and her gloves and bag, which all looked just a little bit on the shabby side, nothing noticeable really. She was quite a lady. It is very seldom we get in anybody who looks even at all worn at the edges, if you follow; and ten to one, if they do, they want to sell, not to buy.

The girl *pulled off* her glove and took out a little tissue paper packet from her bag and laid it on the counter. (I at once noticed her fingers; unusually short for a woman; no wedding ring; nails carelessly varnished; and a split seam in the forefinger of the right glove.)

I undid the packet, and in it there was a cheap paste bracelet.

She said to me: 'Could you mend this for me? The clasp seems to have broken.'

I said: 'I am sorry, madam, we do not do repairs.' (And nor do we, not that sort of junk.)

She hesitated, as though not sure what to do next. Then she just shrugged and said, 'Thank you.' And then—it was very clever the way she did it—her bag just sort of accidentally touched the tissue paper, and it slipped off my side of the counter.

As I *stooped down* to pick it up, I had what I can only regard as a revelation. Everything seemed suddenly clear to me, as though the various bits of a wire puzzle had suddenly slipped into their right places and solved the puzzle for me.

I say everything was clear, but was it? I was certainly not very clear about how to act. At all costs I knew Mr Regnier would want no scene in the shop.

My heart really was in my mouth as I rose up slowly from behind that counter, and no doubt I looked it. I *wrapped* the bracelet *up* in the tissue-paper and handed it back. The girl put it in her bag, and as she turned to go I said to her:

'One moment, please.' But she acted as if she had not heard. So I said quickly, but, of course, quite politely: 'Excuse me, madam, if you do not stop, I shall be compelled to press the alarm and that door in front of you will be locked automatically.' Half-way through I had to swallow. I was so very strung up.

She did stop then, but she did not turn round. Miss Susskind, behind the other counter, stood there like Lot's wife with glasses on.

I came round to the girl and I said: 'We do not want any unpleasantness, madam, either of us. So if you will just hand over the ring in your left hand overcoat pocket the matter will be settled so far as we are concerned. If not, Miss Susskind will press the alarm.'

Miss Susskind nodded when I said this. I could see she was keen to press it anyway.

The girl had gone very pale. I really felt almost sorry for her for the moment, but I knew I had to be firm. She looked at me very frightened, then she *handed over* the ring and ran straight out of the shop.

And at that very minute Mr Regnier came back out of the office with the American customer fully dressed.

The customer was looking all smiles, as though the whole episode was more or less a joke to him. But it was by no means a joke to Mr Regnier. He was all apologies, not smiles.

Then I opened my hand and showed them the ring, and you should have seen Mr Regnier's face, what with seeing his precious ring once more and then seeing the American go flying out of the shop as though a stone from a catapult.

Well, of course, Mr Regnier wondered how on earth I had done it, so I explained.

First of all, we very seldom get any customers like this type of American. Something flashy and more modernistic than our style of jewellery would have been more in his line. He had no taste and what often goes with it—no idea what he really wanted.

Most people who come to us come because they know that at Regnier's you can get the sort of things you cannot just *pick up* anywhere. So query No. one in my mind (not that I had actually got any suspicions up to that moment) was why on earth should they have come to us?

Second point: this was about the girl. Why should anyone hang about in front of an undertaker's? (Of course, at this stage I did not relate the girl with the American customer at all.)

Either one is in need of an undertaker or one is not. It is not a matter that leaves room for doubt in the mind of the ordinary citizen.

So what was this girl doing hanging about in front of the undertaker's? The answer was clear to me; she was killing time. But what for? If her intention was to come to us, why dally in front of an undertaker's?

And then the cheap-looking thing she had brought in for repair. She looked as if she knew what was what, and she was a lady all right. She must have known very well we are not the kind of business that does cheap repairs. All this passed through my mind as I looked at her bracelet.

Point three was this: there was nothing left-handed about her, I had noticed that. Yet it was the left-hand glove she had *pulled off* when she came in, though she had undone the tissue-paper packet with her right. It was at the small counter, and really this counter is only wide enough for one person to stand at conveniently.

The last thing I remembered, as I bent down to pick up the tissue paper, was seeing this girl's left hand at just about the spot where the American had placed his—of course, he was truly left-handed—after I had taken the tray of rings from the safe.

And finally, there was one thing more that had *stuck in my mind*; it stuck rather far back till the critical moment came.

When we had all been crawling about on the carpet, and the American customer looked so cross at Miss Susskind, I remembered noticing he had stopped chewing his gum. Well, you do not just spit gum out on the carpet, even if you are the type of person he was.

And he had not moved a foot either way from where he was standing, so *ipso facto* he must have *disposed of* the gum somewhere within reach, because there was no wastepaper basket, nothing, nowhere, he could have *got rid of* it without one of us would have noticed—except right underneath the ledge of the counter. And that is where I *looked for* the gum, and where I found it just as the girl was about to go out of the shop. And there was the mark on it as clean as a die where the ring had been pressed into it.

It is funny thing the way different people get differently affected by the same things. Mr. Regnier was in such a state, angry, yet most grateful to me,—I really felt quite touched—that he could hardly speak when I told him how the whole thing had happened.

Miss Susskind does not speak much anyway, except to say 'tck, tck,' which she says a hundred times a day if she says it once. And that is exactly what she said.

I suppose I ought to be ashamed to admit it, a man of my age, but when I had finished explaining to Mr Regnier, not only were my hands wringing wet, but I could not stop myself quivering all over for quite a while afterwards. Why?

Nicolas Bentley

Understanding the story

Answer the following questions. Later you may discuss your answers in the class.

1. Where does William Morris work and what job does he do?
2. What are his hobbies?

3. Who are his favorite writers?
4. Why is he interested in detective fiction?
5. Why does he observe people whenever he travels?
6. What is the problem that he faces in his workplace?
7. How does his reading help him in solving the problem at the store?
8. How does he work closely with Miss Susskind and Mr Reginer to solve the problem?

Understanding people

The people in the story have certain special aspects to their characters. Complete the table with the character traits of each person.

Characters	Character traits
1. William Morris	
2. Mr Regnier	
3. Miss Susskind	
4. The American	
5. The girl	

Vocabulary development

Meanings in context

Look up a dictionary and find the meanings of the words and phrases below, as they are used in the context of the story.

Words and phrases	Meanings
1. publican	
2. unobtrusively	
3. antique	
4. undertaker	
5. urn	
6. hearse	
7. disinterested	
8. speculation	
9. arty	
10. in a state	
11. turn-ups	
12. purloined	
13. demur	

14. cranny
15. revelation
16. strung up
17. critical moment
18. ledge

Prepositions

Look at these words. They belong to a group of words called prepositions.

to, from, with, at, in, of, for, about, after, until

Prepositions are words placed before a noun or pronoun to indicate its relation to some other word in a sentence.

For example, in the following phrases, the prepositions are placed before nouns or pronouns.

to Morris, *from* Salford, *with* one daughter, *at* Woldingham, *in* Surrey, *of* the sort, *to* some people

Make a list of at least twenty prepositions. Then fill in the blanks with suitable prepositions and complete the following passages.

1. Joe Larrabee came .... the Middle West. He was a genius .... painting. As a child .... six, he drew a picture .... the town pump .... an important citizen passing it .... a hurry. This effort was framed and hung .... the drugstore window. .... twenty he left .... New York .... a flowing necktie and a small capital.
2. Although Mr McMaster had lived .... Amazonas .... nearly sixty years, no one but a few families .... Shiriana Indians was aware .... his existence. His house stood .... a small savanna, a little patch .... sand and grass three miles or so wide, bounded .... all sides .... forest. Mr McMaster owned a small herd .... cattle, a plantation .... cassava and some banana and mango trees.

Phrasal verbs

Look at the following word groups, which are known as phrasal verbs.

deal with, rely on, look at, make out, come up

These word groups are formed by a verb and a preposition or an adverb. Taken together, the word group has a different meaning from that of the individual words that make up the group.

Look up a dictionary and find the meanings of these phrasal verbs as they are used in the story. They have been italicised in the story so that you can find them easily.

Phrasal verbs	Meanings
1. work off	
2. part with	
3. make up	
4. slip off	
5. warm up	
6. look for	
7. look into	
8. pull off	
9. stoop down	
10. pick up	
11. wrap up	
12. hand over	
13. dispose of	
14. get rid of	

Rewrite the following sentences by replacing the verbs in italics with suitable phrasal verbs.

1. If you *watch* birds carefully, you can soon recognize different species.
2. The American could not *decide* which ring he wanted to buy.
3. Morris *extended* his hand to the American.
4. Morris *kept* the tray on the table.
5. The lady *removed* her glove.
6. The Sub-Inspector *examined* the case seriously.
7. At first, he could not *understand* anything about the case.
8. He *stored* the file safely.
9. He *gave* it to a special officer.
10. The thief, however, *escaped*.

Fixed expressions

Here are some idiomatic expressions that are used in the story. Read the story to understand how they are used. Then use them in sentences of your own.

1. after all 2. at any rate 3. all the same 4. first of all 5. at first glance

Thinking about soft skills

Work in pairs and discuss these questions.

1. What qualities should one possess in order to solve problems?
2. What are some of the steps involved in problem solving?
3. What are the characteristics of an effective solution?

Problem-solving skills from the story

According to the dictionary a problem is a situation, person, or thing that needs to be dealt with or solved. We cannot ignore problems. We have to find the best possible solutions to problems in order to do well at work and live a good life.

Think about the life of the main character in the story, William Morris. He is 53 years old, happily married and has a daughter who is also married. He has a reasonably good job and is contented with his work. But one day he faces a serious problem. An American who visits the shop in which Morris works, attempts to lift a valuable ring with the help of a lady. Cleverly and courageously, Morris is able to solve the problem and restores the ring to his employer.

What skills does he possess? He reads widely and observes people wherever he goes. He is therefore able to develop his powers of observation and deduction. When the theft occurs, he infers from the sequence of events, how the ring must have been taken away by the lady.

William Morris has both interpersonal and intellectual acumen. He has a good relationship with his coworker, Miss Susskind and his employer, Mr Regnier. They understand each other and cooperate effectively to solve the problem of the theft.

There is much that we can learn from the story. If we apply our mind and heart to a problem we can always find workable solutions. We need courage, calmness, and presence of mind to tackle problems.

Activity

Work in groups of four or five. Think of stories from the *Mahabharata* and the *Ramayana*. The manner in which the mythic heroes solved the problems they faced, can help you understand how to deal with problems. Each of you can recount an episode from these epics that highlight problem-solving skills.

Proverbs on problem-solving skills

1. **Read the following proverbs from various countries about the importance of solving problems. Can you add a few more proverbs from your mother tongue or any other**

language? Which proverb do you like the most? Why? Share your views with the class.

a. Every cloud has a silver lining.
b. God helps those who help themselves.
c. There is no use crying over spilt milk.
d. Where there is a will there is a way.
e. Necessity is the mother of invention.
f. The squeaky wheel gets the grease.
g. When you see an arrow that is not going to miss you, throw out your chest and meet it head on.
h. There are no cakes without work.

2. **These proverbs point to the fact that every problem has a solution provided we are willing to work hard to find a solution. Write a paragraph of about 150 words discussing the skills required to solve problems effectively.**

Soft skills at the workplace

Work in groups and discuss the following situations.

1. In the course of your life as an employee, you may find that something goes missing from your custody. You are responsible for what has been lost. What will you do in such a situation?
2. How does each of these help you in solving problems?
   a. attending workshops and seminars to keep you up to date with developments in your area of work
   b. reading literature relevant to your industry
   c. developing sharp observation skills

Real life experience

You may have known or heard about an attempted theft in a jewellery showroom. Write a paragraph in about 150 words on how the stolen jewellery was recovered.

Self-assessment

Read the following 'yes' or 'no' questions carefully. If your answer is YES, write 1. If your answer is NO, write 0.

	Questions	1 or 0
1.	Do you assess situations and identify problems?	
2.	Do you seek different points of view and evaluate them based on facts?	
3.	Do you recognize the human, interpersonal, technical, scientific, and mathematical dimensions of a problem?	
4.	Do you identify the root cause of a problem?	
5.	Do you explore possible solutions creatively and innovatively?	
6.	Do you readily use science, technology, and mathematics as a way to think, gain and share knowledge, solve problems and make decisions?	
7.	Do you evaluate solutions to make recommendations or decisions?	
8.	Do you implement solutions?	
9.	Do you check to see if a solution works, and act on opportunities for improvement?	
10.	Do you extract the maximum information from facts?	
11.	Do you collect information from more than one source?	
12.	Do you look for a pattern in the facts you collect?	
13.	Do you understand events and their relationships in time?	
14.	Do you have the ability to organise information properly?	
15.	Do you give logical reasons for opinions?	
16.	Do you relate information to possible outcomes?	
17.	Do you plan future actions?	
18.	Do you regulate and plan your responses?	
19.	Do you have the confidence to fail?	
20.	Do you understand the importance of the process as well as the outcome in problem solving?	

If your score is between 15–20, you have excellent problem solving skills. If your score is less than 15, you have to improve your problem solving skills.

Further reading

Here are three collections of stories by Nicolas Bentley. Read the stories and if possible, discuss them in the class.

1. The Tongue-Tied Canary
2. How Can You Bear To be Human?
3. Trent's Few Cases

7. Interview Skills

Leading up to the story

Discuss these questions in groups of four or five. The group leader may then present the answers to the class.

1. What is a lighthouse?
2. According to you, what qualifications should a lighthouse keeper have?
3. When would an adventurous person want to settle down to a quiet life?

The lighthouse keeper of Aspinwall

Read the story by Henryk Sienkiewicz. Then answer the questions that follow.

On a time it happened that the lighthouse keeper in Aspinwall, not far from Panama, disappeared without a trace. Since he disappeared during a storm, it was supposed that the ill-fated man went to the very edge of the small, rocky island on which the lighthouse stood, and was swept out by a wave. This supposition seemed the more likely as his boat was not found next day in its rocky niche. The place of lighthouse keeper had become vacant. It was necessary to fill this place at the earliest moment possible, since the lighthouse had no small significance for the local movement as well as for vessels going from New York to Panama. Mosquito Bay abounds in sandbars and banks. Among these navigation, even in the daytime, is difficult; but at night, especially with the fogs which are so frequent on those waters warmed by the sun of the tropics, it is nearly impossible. The only guide at that time for the numerous vessels is the lighthouse.

The task of finding a new keeper fell to the United States consul living in Panama, and this task was no small one: first, because it was absolutely necessary to find the man within twelve hours; second, the man must be unusually conscientious, it was not possible, of course, to take the first comer at random; finally, there was an utter lack of candidates. Life on a tower is uncommonly difficult, and by no means enticing to people of the South, who love idleness and the freedom of a vagrant life*. That lighthouse keeper is almost a prisoner. He cannot leave his rocky island except on Sundays. A boat from

* A stereotype which is no longer acceptable today.

Aspinwall brings him provisions and water once a day, and returns immediately; on the whole island, one acre in area, there is no inhabitant. The keeper lives in the lighthouse; he keeps it in order. During the day he gives signals by displaying flags of various colours to indicate changes of the barometer; in the evening he lights the lantern. This would be no great labour were it not that to reach the lantern at the summit of the tower he must pass over more than four hundred steep and very high steps; sometimes he must make this journey repeatedly during the day. In general, it is the life of a monk, and indeed more than that, the life of a hermit. It was not wonderful, therefore, that Mr. Isaac Falconbridge was in no small anxiety as to where he should find a permanent successor to the recent keeper; and it is easy to understand his joy when a successor announced himself most unexpectedly on that very day. He was a man already old, seventy years or more, but fresh, erect, with the movements and bearing of a soldier. His hair was perfectly white, his face as dark as that of a Creole; but, judging from his blue eyes, he did not belong to a people of the South. His face was somewhat downcast and sad, but honest. At the first glance he pleased Falconbridge. It remained only to examine him. Therefore the following conversation began:

'Where are you from?'

'I am a Pole.'

'Where have you worked up to this time?'

'In one place and another.'

'A lighthouse keeper should like to stay in one place.'

'I need rest.'

'Have you served? Have you testimonials of honourable government service?'

The old man drew from his bosom a piece of faded silk resembling a strip of an old flag, unwound it, and said:

'Here are the testimonials. I received this cross in 1830. This second one is Spanish from the Carlist War; the third is the French legion; the fourth I received in Hungary. Afterward I fought in the States against the South; there they do not give crosses.'

Falconbridge took the paper and began to read.

'H'm! Skavinski? Is that your name? H'm! Two flags captured in a bayonet attack. You were a gallant soldier.'

'I am able to be a conscientious lighthouse keeper.'

'It is necessary to ascend the tower a number of times daily. Have you sound legs?'

'I crossed the plains on foot.' (The immense steppes between the East and California are called 'the plains.')

'Do you know sea service?'

'I served three years on a whaler.'

'You have tried various occupations.'

'The only one I have not known is quiet.'

'Why is that?'

The old man shrugged his shoulders. 'Such is my fate.'

'Still you seem to me too old for a lighthouse keeper.'

'Sir,' exclaimed the candidate suddenly in a voice of emotion, 'I am greatly wearied, knocked about. I have passed through much as you see. This place is one of those which I have wished for most ardently. I am old, I need rest. I need to say to myself, 'Here you will remain; this is your port.' Ah, sir, this depends now on you alone. Another time perhaps such a place will not offer itself. What luck that I was in Panama! I entreat you—as God is dear to me, I am like a ship which if it misses the harbour will be lost. If you wish to make an old man happy—I swear to you that I am honest, but—I have enough of wandering.'

The blue eyes of the old man expressed such earnest entreaty that Falconbridge, who had a good, simple heart, was touched.

'Well,' said he, 'I take you. You are lighthouse keeper.'

The old man's face gleamed with inexpressible joy.

'I thank you.'

'Can you go to the tower today?'

'I can.'

'Then good-bye. Another word,—for any failure in service you will be dismissed.'

'All right.'

That same evening, when the sun had descended on the other side of the isthmus, and a day of sunshine was followed by a night without twilight, the new keeper was in his place evidently, for the lighthouse was casting its bright rays on the water as usual. The night was perfectly calm, silent, genuinely tropical, filled with a transparent haze, forming around the moon a great colored rainbow with soft, unbroken edges; the sea was moving only because the tide raised it. Skavinski on the balcony seemed from below like a small black point. He tried to collect his thoughts and take in his new position; but his mind was too much under pressure to move with regularity. He felt somewhat as a hunted beast feels when at last it has found refuge from pursuit on some inaccessible rock or in a cave. There had come to him, finally, an hour of quiet; the feeling of safety filled his soul with a certain unspeakable bliss. Now on that rock he can simply laugh at his previous wanderings, his misfortunes and failures. He was in truth like a ship whose masts, ropes, and sails had been broken and rent by a tempest, and cast from the clouds to the bottom of the sea,—a ship on which the tempest had hurled waves and spat foam, but which still wound its way to the harbour. The pictures of that storm passed quickly through his mind as he compared it with the calm future now beginning. A part of his wonderful adventures he had related to Falconbridge; he had not mentioned, however, thousands of other incidents. It had been his misfortune that as often as he pitched his tent and fixed his fireplace to settle down permanently, some wind tore out the stakes of his tent, whirled away the fire, and bore him on toward destruction. Looking now from the balcony of the tower at the illuminated waves, he remembered everything through which he had passed. He had campaigned in the four parts of the world, and in wandering had tried almost every occupation.

Labour-loving and honest, more than once had he earned money, and had always lost it in spite of every prevision and the utmost caution. He had been a gold-miner in Australia, a diamond-digger in Africa, a rifleman in public service in the East Indies. He established a ranch in California,—the drought ruined him; he tried trading with wild tribes in the interior of Brazil,— his raft was wrecked on the Amazon; he himself alone, weaponless, and nearly naked, wandered in the forest for many weeks living on wild fruits, exposed every moment to death from the jaws of wild beasts. He established a forge in Helena, Arkansas, and that was burned in a great fire which consumed the whole town. Next he fell into the hands of Indians in the Rocky Mountains, and only through a miracle was he saved by Canadian trappers. Then he served as a sailor on a vessel running between Bahia and Bordeaux, and as harpooner on a whaling-ship; both vessels were wrecked. He had a cigar factory in Havana, and was robbed by his partner while he himself was lying sick with the vomito. At last he came to Aspinwall, and there was to be the end of his failures,—for what could reach him on that rocky island? Neither water nor fire nor men. But from men Skavinski had not suffered much; he had met good men oftener than bad ones.

But it seemed to him that all the four elements were persecuting him. Those who knew him said that he had no luck, and with that they explained everything. He himself became somewhat of a monomaniac. He believed that some mighty and vengeful hand was pursuing him everywhere, on all lands and waters. He did not like, however, to speak of this; only at times, when some one asked him whose hand that could be, he pointed mysteriously to the Polar Star, and said, 'It comes from that place.'In reality his failures were so continuous that they were wonderful, and might easily drive a nail into the head, especially of the man who had experienced them. But Skavinski had the patience of an Indian, and that great calm power of resistance which comes from truth of heart. In his time he had received in Hungary a number of bayonet-thrusts because he would not grasp at a stirrup which was shown as means of salvation to him, and cry for quarter. In like manner he did not bend to misfortune. He crept up against the mountain as industriously as an ant. Pushed down a hundred times, he began his journey calmly for the hundred and first time. He was in his way a most peculiar original. This old soldier, tempered, God knows in how many fires, hardened in suffering, hammered and forged, had the heart of a child. In the time of the epidemic in Cuba, the vomito attacked him because he had given to the sick all his quinine, of which he had a considerable supply, and left not a grain to himself.

There had been in him also this wonderful quality, — that after so many disappointments he was ever full of confidence, and did not lose hope that all would be well yet. In winter he grew lively, and predicted great events. He waited for these events with impatience, and lived with the thought of them whole summers. But the winters passed one after another, and Skavinski lived only to this,—that they whitened his head. At last he grew old, began to lose energy; his endurance was becoming more and more like resignation, his former calmness was tending toward super-sensitiveness, and that tempered soldier was degenerating into a man ready to shed tears for any cause. Besides this, from time to time he was weighed down by a terrible homesickness which was roused by any circumstance,—the sight of swallows, gray birds like sparrows, snow on the mountains, or melancholy music like that heard on a time. Finally, there was one idea which mastered him,—the idea of rest. It mastered the old man thoroughly, and swallowed all other desires and hopes. This ceaseless wanderer could not imagine anything more to be longed for, anything more precious, than a quiet corner in which to rest, and wait in silence for the end. Perhaps specially because some whim of fate had so hurried him over all seas and lands that he could hardly catch his breath, did he imagine that the highest human happiness was simply not to wander. It is true that such modest happiness was his due; but he was so accustomed to disappointments that he thought of rest as people in general think of something which is beyond reach. He did not dare to hope for it.

Meanwhile, unexpectedly, in the course of twelve hours he had gained a position which was as if chosen for him out of all the world. We are not to wonder, then, that when he lighted his lantern in the evening he became as it were dazed,—that he asked himself if that was reality, and he did not dare to answer that it was. But at the same time reality convinced him with incontrovertible proofs; hence hours one after another passed while he was on the balcony. He gazed, and convinced himself. It might seem that he was looking at the sea for the first time in his life. The lens of the lantern cast into the darkness an enormous triangle of light, beyond which the eye of the old man was lost in the black distance completely, in the distance mysterious and awful. But that distance seemed to run toward the light. The long waves following one another rolled out from the darkness, and went bellowing toward the base of the island; and then their foaming backs were visible, shining rose-colored in the light of the lantern. The incoming tide swelled more and more, and covered the sandy bars. The mysterious speech of the ocean came with a fullness more powerful and louder, at one time like the thunder of cannon, at another like the roar of great forests, at another like the distant dull sound of the voices of people. At moments it was quiet; then to the ears of the old man came some great sigh, then a kind of sobbing, and again threatening outbursts.

At last the wind bore away the haze, but brought black, broken clouds, which hid the moon. From the west it began to blow more and more; the waves sprang with rage against the rock of the lighthouse, licking with foam the foundation walls. In the distance a storm was beginning to bellow. On the dark, disturbed expanse certain green lanterns gleamed from the masts of ships. These green points rose high and then sank; now they swayed to the right, and now to the left. Skavinski descended to his room. The storm began to howl. Outside, people on those ships were struggling with night, with darkness, with waves; but inside the tower it was calm and still. Even the sounds of the storm hardly came through the thick walls, and only the measured tick-tack of the clock lulled the wearied old man to his slumber.

Henryk Sienkiewicz
(from 'The Lighthouse Keeper of Aspinwall')

Understanding the story

Answer the following questions. Later you may discuss your answers in the class.

1. How did the lighthouse keeper's job fall vacant?
2. Why is it important to find a suitable candidate for the job in twelve hours?
3. Who is the employer?
4. What is the nature of the job?
5. How does the interview begin, develop, and conclude?
6. Which question is the most challenging one for Skavinski?
7. How does Skavinski answer this question?
8. What are his strengths and weaknesses?
9. What does Skavinski achieve when he gets the job?
10. Why does Skavinski not share some of the most difficult incidents of his life with his employer?
11. What qualities of Skavinski does the author admire?
12. Do you think Skavinski will remain at the lighthouse or will he resume his travelling?

Understanding people

There are two main characters in the story. Identify the special qualities which define each of them and complete the table.

Characters	Special qualities
1. Skavinski	
2. US Consul	

Understanding the world

Skavinski had worked in many parts of the world. Name the places and what he did there, and complete the table.

Places	Skavinski's activities
1.	
2.	
3.	
4.	
5.	
6.	
7.	
8.	
9.	
10.	

Vocabulary development

Meanings in context

Look up a dictionary and find the meanings of the words and phrases below, as they are used in the context of the story.

Words and phrases	Meanings
1. supposition	
2. vessels	
3. Creole	
4. conscientious	
5. ardently	
6. isthmus	
7. tempest	
8. ranch	
9. forge	
10. harpooner	
11. persecuting	
12. monomaniac	
13. salvation	
14. quinine	
15. melancholy	
16. incontrovertible	

Conjunctions

Read the extract below.

> *Since* he disappeared during a storm, it was supposed that the ill-fated man went to the very edge of the small, rocky island on which the lighthouse stood, *and* was swept out by a wave. This supposition seemed the more likely *as* his boat was not found next day in its rocky niche. The place of lighthouse keeper had become vacant. It was necessary to fill this place at the earliest moment possible, *since* the lighthouse had no small significance for the local movement *as well as* for vessels going from New York to Panama. Mosquito Bay abounds in sandbars and banks. Among these navigation, even in the daytime, is difficult; *but* at night, especially with the fogs which are so frequent on those waters warmed by the sun of the tropics, it is nearly impossible. The only guide at that time for the numerous vessels is the lighthouse.

The words in italics are called conjunctions. They link words, phrases and parts of sentences with each other. There are three kinds of conjunctions in English: coordinating, subordinating, and correlative.

Coordinating conjunctions

There are seven coordinating conjunctions: *for*, *and*, *nor*, *but*, *or*, *yet*, and *so*. We use them to convey these meanings: *but* for contrast, *so* and *for* for reason, *and* for addition, *or* for choice, *nor* for negative choice, and *yet* for concession.

Look at the examples below to understand how they are used.

- The US consul had to find the new lighthouse keeper. He had to find him soon. The US consul had to find the new lighthouse keeper *and* he had to find him soon.
- Skavinski suffered from the vomito. He gave all his quinine to poor people. Skavinski suffered from the vomito, *yet* he gave all his quinine to poor people.
- He was an old man. He had enough strength to work as lighthouse keeper. He was an old man *but* had enough strength to work as a lighthouse keeper.

Combine the following pairs of sentences with coordinating conjunctions.

1. Sanjeev is a singer. He knows how to play the violin.
2. Maya did not do very well in her plus two examination. She could not get admission in the college of her choice.
3. Akila is a physically challenged girl. She does not want sympathy from anybody.

4. You are interested in engineering. You are studying medicine.
5. Wipro has a branch in New York. My supervisor has planned to send me there for three months.

Subordinating conjunctions

There are a large number of subordinating conjunctions in English. Here are some commonly used subordinating conjunctions.

though, although, even though, since, as, because, if, unless, until, till, after, before, when, whereas, while

Look at the following examples to understand how they are used.

- The old lighthouse keeper had disappeared without a trace. A new lighthouse keeper had to be appointed immediately.
  Since the old lighthouse keeper had disappeared without a trace, a new lighthouse keeper had to be appointed immediately.
- Skavinski was old. The US consul found him suitable for the job.
  Though Skavinski was old, the US consul found him suitable for the job.
- Skavinski was restless. He got the job of the lighthouse keeper.
  Skavinski was restless *until* he got the job of the lighthouse keeper.

Combine the following pairs of sentences with subordinating conjunctions.

1. Latha studied maths in high school. She did not choose engineering.
2. Sachin has played cricket brilliantly for decades. The Government of India has awarded him the Padma Bhushan.
3. Your colleague does not cooperate with you. Reason with her instead of raising your voice.
4. Engineering students get dream jobs. They hone their skills in finishing schools.
5. You want to become an administrator. You need to do an MBA from a reputed university.

Correlative conjunctions

Conjunctions which are used in pairs to show a relationship between different parts of a sentence are called correlative conjunctions. Here are some commonly used correlative conjunctions.

whether ... or, either ... or, neither ... nor, not only ... but also, both ... and

Look at the following examples to understand how they are used.

- He is a dancer or he is a musician. I do not know.
  I do not know *whether* he is a dancer *or* a musician.

- He may be an engineer. Or he may be a doctor.
  He may be *either* an engineer *or* a doctor.

- Our college is not funded by the government. It is not funded by donations from individuals.
  Our college is funded *neither* by the government *nor* by donations from individuals.

- IT industries consider Tamilnadu a preferred destination. Automobile industries also consider Tamilnadu a preferred destination.
  Not only IT industries *but also* automobile industries consider Tamilnadu a preferred destination.

- Employers want to have students with good communication skills. They also want to have students with good technical knowledge.
  Employers want to have students who have *both* good communication skills *and* technical knowledge.

Combine the following pairs of sentences with correlative conjunctions

1. You can check the internet or a reference book. It does not matter.
2. You can finish your field work this month. Or you can finish it the next month.
3. The manager will be at the meeting. The employees will be at the meeting.
4. Good colleges require you to pass an exam. They also want you to pass an interview.
5. You cannot choose French as a second language. You cannot choose German as a second language.

Using words accurately

Read the following sentence from the text

'In general, it is the life of a monk, and indeed more than that,—the life of a hermit.'

The author tries to distinguish between the words, 'monk' and 'hermit'. Look up a dictionary and find out the difference in their meaning.

Bring out the difference in meaning in the pairs of words below by using them in sentences of your own.

1. engineer and technologist
2. accountant and finance officer

3. physicist and physician
4. doctor and surgeon
5. island and archipelago
6. sea and ocean
7. lane and avenue
8. beach and shore
9. journal and magazine
10. company and firm

Thinking about soft skills

Work in pairs and discuss these questions.

1. What things do you carry with you to an interview?
2. Why is the first impression very important?
3. What are the various sources of information about jobs?

Interview skills from the story

Skavinski displays excellent interview skills during his meeting with Falconbridge for the job of lighthouse keeper. Before he attends the interview, he does his groundwork well. He studies the job requirements and decides that the job suits him. The job needs a person willing to live like a prisoner, with little contact with the outside world, and Skavinsky fits the bill because he needs rest. The job requires that the person have the courage and confidence to live alone. Skavinski has these qualities. In addition, Skaninky is well-prepared for the interview. He takes his credentials with him and produces them at the right time during the interview. He explains why he does not have any certificate for his participation in the war against the South. He also defends himself firmly but politely against his old age being perceived as a weakness.

Skavinski's non-verbal communication skills are excellent too. During the interview, his earnestness and sincerity of purpose is clearly visible to his employer and he is able to convince Falconbridge to hire him.

Activity

1. **A job application usually contains three elements: covering letter, résumé, and copies of your certificates.**

Imagine you have completed your degree course and you are applying for the post of manager in an automobile company. Write a covering letter and then prepare a résumé. Mention the enclosures related to your certificates in the covering letter. A general format common to many sectors is given below.

Sample Cover Letter

III/3, Rams Flats
I Main Road, Gandhi Nagar
Adyar, Chennai – 600 020
Cell: 9786686650
rmrnagaragan@gmail.com

15 April 2010

The General Manager
Maruti Motors and Technologies
Mahatma Gandhi Road
Cochin – 682065.

Dear Sir,

Subject: Application for the post of production manager

This is with reference to your advertisement in The Hindu, dated 7 March 2010, for the job of production manager in your organisation.

Currently, I am working as an assistant engineer in the production department of Hyundai Motors. As assistant engineer in the production department, I am in charge of leading the team of technical supervisors in the Adyar branch. My job profile requires me to motivate the supervisors to maintain the highest technical standards as well as provide them with on the spot technical support. My job demands that I keep in touch with current developments in the industry.

My ability to work with people and my familiarity with emerging technologies make me believe that I will be able to contribute favourably to the growth of your organisation.

I enclose copies of my school, college and experience certificates.

I look forward to hearing from you.

Yours sincerely,

Nagarajan, Rm. R

Enclosure: as stated

Sample Résumé

NAGARAJAN, Rm. R
III/3, Rams Flats
I Main Road, Gandhi Nagar
Adyar, Chennai – 600 020
Cell: 9786686650
rmrnagaragan@gmail.com

Career objective:

To obtain the job of a production manager in organisation where people skills and technical knowledge can contribute to increased productivity.

Skills summary:

Adaptable, willing to work in teams, strong analytical skills and interpersonal skills
Working knowledge of Malayalam, German, and French
Programming in C, C++, Basic, and Java

Education and training:

B.E. in Manufacturing Engineering, First Class, NITT, May 2008
PG Diploma in Manufacturing Engineering from the University of South Wales, June 2009

Work History:

Hyundai Motors, Chennai, July 2009 to the present
Assistant Engineer, in-charge of production plant

Reference:

Mr R K Rajaram
Executive Engineer
Hyundai Motors
Bangalore Highway
Chennai – 600 125
Mobile: 9444019867
Email: rkr@hyundai.com

2. **Role play the following scenarios.**
   a. Work in pairs with one student taking on the role of Skavinsky and the other, the role of Falconbridge. Enact the interview situation in the story.
   b. Work in groups of four. One student in the group will be a candidate and the rest will be interview panel members. Conduct mock interviews for jobs in different sectors.

Proverbs on interview skills

1. **Read the following proverbs from various countries which deal with how to conduct yourself at interviews. Can you add a few more proverbs from your mother tongue or any other language? Which proverb do you like the most? Why? Share your views with the class.**
   a. When you meet a man, you judge him by his clothes; when you leave, you judge him by his heart.
   b. He who is outside the door has already a good part of his journey behind him.
   c. Opportunity seldom knocks twice.
   d. Where there is no vision, people perish.
   e. There are no traffic jams when you go the extra mile.
   f. A happy face is the sign of a good heart.
   g. When one door closes another door opens.
   h. You cannot chase two antelopes at once.
   i. The journey of a thousand miles begins with a single step.
   j. Honesty is the best policy.

2. **This set of proverbs gives you an insight into how an interview must be approached by both the interviewer and the candidate being interviewed. For example, the first proverb points to how interviewers judge a candidate, the fifth proverb tells you that reaching the venue well in advance will save you from traffic jams on the way, and the last proverb tells you that answering questions honestly is expected of every candidate.**

   Using the proverbs as a guide, write a paragraph in about 150 words on the importance of interview skills.

Soft skills at the workplace

Here are some activities you can do to develop your interview skills.

1. Invite college alumni who have successful careers to address your class. Ask questions on how to improve your interview skills.

2. Ask your teachers to share their own interview experiences.
3. Work in groups and make a list of all the things you must do when you appear for an interview. Share your lists with the class.
4. After an interview is over, you too may want to ask the interviewer some questions.
   Work in pairs and make a list of questions you could ask the interviewer.

Real life experience

Speak to family members or friends and ask them to recall their experiences of interviews. If they tell you something interesting, you may want to share it with your class.

Self-assessment

Read the following 'yes' or 'no' questions carefully. If your answer is YES, write 1. If your answer is NO, write 0.

	Questions	1 or 0
1.	Do you know your personal and professional goals?	
2.	Do you know your strengths and weaknesses?	
3.	Do you gather adequate information about the company and the job you apply for?	
4.	Do you prepare for the interview thoroughly?	
5.	Do you practice well for the interview?	
6.	Do you dress neatly for the interview?	
7.	Do you take all necessary documents with you?	
8.	Do you take additional copies of your latest résumé with you?	
9.	Do you reach the venue well in advance?	
10.	Do you greet the panel members at the interview?	
11.	Do you thank the panel members for permitting you to take your seat?	
12.	Do you introduce yourself clearly and concisely?	
13.	Do you maintain eye contact with the panel members?	
14.	Do you listen well and answer questions to the point?	
15.	Do you speak confidently and clearly?	
16.	Do you maintain a cheerful manner?	
17.	Do you answer questions honestly?	
18.	Do you ask relevant questions?	

19. Do you close the interview with thanks for the opportunity?
20. Do you write a note of thanks to the HR department after the interview?
21. Do you continue to keep in touch with the HR department, even if you are not selected?

If your score is between 15-21, you have excellent interview skills. If your score is less than 15, you have to improve your interview skills.

Further reading

The story given here is only the first part of a larger story. It has two other parts. You may read them to know how the story ends and what happens to the main character. You can find the story at the website [http://www.readbookonline.net/readOnLine/1447/]

Here are the names of two more stories by Henryk Sienkiewicz:
'Yamiol,'
'Janko the Musician.'
Read the stories and discuss them in the class.

8. Adaptability Skills

Leading up to the story

Discuss these questions in groups of four or five. The group leader may then present the answers to the class.

1. Why do employees sometimes take an advance against their salaries?
2. Why is it essential for employers to understand the needs of their employees?
3. What are some of the ways in which the management of an organisation can win the trust of its employees?

Señor Payroll

Read the story by W E Barrett. Then answer the questions that follow.

Larry and I were Junior Engineers in the gas plant, which means that we were clerks. Anything that could be classified as paper work came to the flat double desk across which we faced each other. The main office downtown sent us a bewildering array of orders and rules that were to be put into effect.

Junior Engineers were beneath the notice of everyone except the Mexican labourers at the plant. To them we were the visible form of a distant, unknowable paymaster. We were Señor Payroll.

Those Mexicans were great workmen: the aristocrats among them were the stokers, big men who worked Herculean eight-hour shifts in the fierce heat of the retorts. They scooped coal with huge shovels and hurled it with uncanny aim at tiny doors. The coal streamed out from the shovels like black water from a high pressure nozzle, and never missed the narrow opening. The stokers worked stripped to the waist, and there was pride and dignity in them. Few men could do such work, and they were the few.

The Company paid its men only twice a month, on the fifth and on the twentieth. To a Mexican, this was absurd. What man with money will make it last fifteen days? If he hoarded money beyond the spending of three days, he was a miser—and when, Señor, did the blood of Spain flow in the veins of misers? Hence it was the custom for our stokers to appear every third or fourth day to draw the money due to them.

There was a certain elasticity in the Company rules, and Larry and I sent the necessary forms to the Main Office and received an 'advance' against a man's pay check. Then, one day, Downtown favored us with a memorandum:

'There have been too many abuses of the advance-against-wages privilege. Hereafter, no advance against wages will be made to any employee except in a case of genuine emergency.'

We had no sooner posted the notice when in came stoker Juan Garcia. He asked for an advance. I pointed to the notice. He spelled it through slowly, then, said, 'What does this mean, this "genuine emergency"?'

I explained to him patiently that the Company was kind and sympathetic, but that it was a great nuisance to have to pay wages every few days. If someone was ill or if money was urgently needed for some other good reason, then the Company would make an exception to the rule.

Juan Garcia turned his hat over and over slowly in his big hands. 'I do not get my money?'

'Next payday, Juan. On the Twentieth.'

He went out silently and I felt a little ashamed of myself. I looked across the desk at Larry. He avoided my eyes.

In the next hour two other stokers came in, looked at the notice, had it explained and walked solemnly out; then no more came. What we did not know was that Juan Garcia, Pete Mendoza and Francisco Gonzalez had spread the word and that every Mexican in the plant was explaining the order to every other Mexican. 'To get the money now, the wife must be sick. There must be medicine for the baby.'

The next morning Juan Garcia's wife was practically dying, Pete Mendonza's mother would hardly last the day, there was a veritable epidemic among children and, just for variety, there was one sick father. We always suspected that the old man was really sick; no Mexican would otherwise have thought of him. At any rate, nobody paid Larry and me to examine private lives; we made out our forms with an added line describing the 'genuine emergency.' Our people got paid.

That went on for a week. Then came a new order, curt and to the point: 'Hereafter, employees will be paid only on the fifth and the twentieth of the month. No exceptions will be made except in the cases of employees leaving the service of the Company.' The notice went up on the board and we explained its significance gravely. 'No Juan Garcia, we cannot advance your wages. It is too bad about your wife and your cousins and your aunts, but there is a new rule.'

Juan Garcia went out and thought it over. He thought out loud with Mendoza and Gonzalez and Ayala, then, in the morning, he was back. 'I am quitting this company for different job. You pay me now?'

We argued that it was a good company and that it loved its employees like children, but in the end we paid off, because Juan Garcia quit. And so did Gonzalez, Mendoza Obregon, Ayala and Ortez, the best stokers, men who could not be replaced. Larry and I looked at each other; we knew what was coming in about three days. One of our duties was to sit on the hiring line early each morning, engaging transient workers for the handy gangs. Any man was accepted who could walk up and ask for a job without falling down. Never before had we been called upon to hire such skilled virtuosos as stokers for handy-gang work, but we were called upon to hire them now.

The day foreman was wringing his hands and asking the Almighty if he was personally supposed to shovel this condemned coal, while there in a stolid, patient line were skilled men—'Garcia, Mendoza and others'—waiting to be hired. We hired them, of course. There was nothing else to do.

Every day we had a line of resigning stokers, and another line of stokers seeking work. Our paper work became very complicated. At the Main Office they were jumping up and down. The procession of forms showing Juan Garcia's resigning and being hired over and over again was too much for them. Sometimes Downtown had Garcia on the payroll twice at the same time when someone down there was slow in entering a resignation. Our phone rang early and often.

Tolerantly and patiently we were explaining: 'There's nothing we can do if a man wants to quit, and if there are stokers available when the plant needs stokers, we hire them.'

Out of chaos, Downtown issued another order. I read it and whistled. Larry looked at it and said, 'It is going to be very quiet around here.'

The order read: 'Hereafter, no employee who resigns may be rehired within a period of thirty days.'

Juan Garcia was due for another resignation, and when he came in we showed him the order and explained that standing in line the next day would do him no good if he resigned today. 'Thirty days is a long time, Juan.'

It was a grave matter and he took time to reflect on it. So did Gonzalez, Mendoza, Ayala and Ortez. Ultimately, however, they were all back — and all resigned.

We did our best to dissuade them and we were sad about the parting. This time it was for keeps and they shook hands with us solemnly. It was very nice knowing us. Larry and I looked at each other when they were gone and we both knew that neither of us had been pulling for Downtown to win this duel. It was a blue day.

In the morning, however, they were all back in line. With the utmost gravity, Juan Garcia informed me that he was a stoker looking for a job.

'No dice, Juan,' I said. 'Come back in 30 days.' I warned you.

His eyes looked straight into mine without a flicker. 'There is some mistake, Señor,' he said. 'I am Manual Hernandez. I work as the stoker in Pueblo, in Santa Fe, in many places.'

I stared back at him, remembering the sick wife and the babies without medicine, the mother-in-law in the hospital, the many resignations and the rehirings. I knew that there was a gas plant in Pueblo, and that there was not any in Santa Fe; but who was I to argue with a man about his own name? A stoker is a stoker.

So I hired him. I hired Gonzalez, too, who swore that his name was Carrera, and Ayala, who had shamelessly become Smith.

Three days later, the resigning started.

Within a week our payroll read like a history of Latin America. Everyone was on it: Lopez and Obregon, Villa, Diaz, Batista, Gomez, and even San Martin and Bolivar. Finally Larry and I, growing weary of staring at familiar faces and writing unfamiliar names, went to the Superintendent and told the whole story. He tried not to grin, and said, 'Damned nonsense!'

The next day the orders were taken down. We called our most prominent stokers into the office and pointed to the board. No rules any more.

'The next time we hire you hombres,' Larry said grimly, 'come in under the names you like best, because, that's the way you are going to stay on the books.'

They looked at us and they looked at the board: then for the first time in the long duel, their teeth flashed white. 'Si, Señores,' they said.

And so it was.

William E. Barrett

Understanding the story

Answer the following questions. Later you may discuss your answers in the class.

1. What is the job responsibility of the two junior engineers?
2. What qualities do the stokers have that make them indispensable to the company?
3. What system of wage payment does the gas company have?
4. Why did the company issue the first memo?
5. Why did the stokers start to make up excuses?
6. Why did they start resigning?
7. Why did they start assuming different names?
8. What did the company finally do?
9. Why did a situation of conflict develop?
10. Who benefited when the conflict was resolved?

Understanding people

There are a number of characters in the story. The action of one character causes another character to respond. For example, the management's first memorandum resulted in the stokers making up 'emergencies' in order to get an advance.

Complete the table by filling in the actions taken by various characters and the responses to each of them.

	Actions of the characters	Responses
1.	The management's first memorandum	Stokers make up emergencies
2.		
3.		
4.		
5.		

Understanding organisational communication

There are three main types of organisational communication. When information flows downward to employees through various middle levels of management, it is called top-down communication. When the employees send information to the top management via different levels of middle management, it is known as upward communication. The third type of communication relates to the free flow of information among people of the same level or rank in an organisation. This is called lateral or diagonal communication.

Answer the following questions.

1. Which types of communication do you find in the story?
2. How can the gas company improve its communication and its productivity?
3. Which type of communication is good for an organisation?

Vocabulary development

Meanings in context

Look up a dictionary and find the meanings of the words and phrases below, as they are used in the context of the story.

	Words and phrases	Meanings
1.	downtown	
2.	bewildering	
3.	stokers	
4.	retorts	
5.	scooped	
6.	uncanny	
7.	nozzle	

8. absurd
9. elasticity
10. vertitable
11. curt
12. transient
13. virtuosos
14. stolid
15. dissuade
16. hombres

Active voice and passive voice

Look at the words in italics in the following sentences.

- Larry and the narrator *managed* the stokers.
- The main office *sent* us a bewildering array of orders.

These words are verbs which take an object after them. For example, the verb *managed* is followed by the object, *stokers* and the verb *sent* is followed by the object, *orders*. They are known as transitive verbs. Such verbs can take either the active voice or the passive voice. When the subject of the sentence performs or causes the action, the verb takes the active voice. For example, in the first sentence, 'Larry and the manager' (the subject of the sentence) perform the action. Therefore the sentence is in the active voice. Similarly, in the second sentence, 'the main office' (the subject of the sentence) performs the action. Both sentences are in the active voice. Look at the examples below to understand how they can be changed to the passive voice.

- Larry and the narrator managed the stokers.
  The stokers were managed by Larry and the narrator.
- The main office sent us a bewildering array of orders.
  We were sent a bewildering array of orders by the main office.
  Or
  A bewildering array of orders was sent to us by the main office.

1. Change the following sentences from the active to the passive voice.

a. We implemented the orders.
b. They scooped coal with huge shovels and hurled it with uncanny aim at tiny doors.

c. The company paid its men only twice a month.
d. So I hired Juan.
e. They called the most prominent stokers into the office.

When the subject of the sentence is acted upon by the object, the verb takes the passive voice. In the sentence below, 'the student', (the subject of the sentence) is acted upon by the object, 'the teacher'. The sentence is therefore in the passive voice. Look at the example below to understand how to change a sentence from the passive to the active voice.

Passive voice: The student was encouraged by the teacher to improve her adaptability skills.

Active voice: The teacher encouraged the student to improve her adaptability skills.

2. Change the following sentences to the active voice.

a. The employees were appreciated by the manager for their cooperation.
b. The children were given scholarships for higher studies.
c. A new health insurance scheme has been announced by the government.
d. The unemployed youth is being taken care of by the employment guarantee programme.
e. The oil companies had been told not to increase the price of oil until further orders.

Direct and indirect speech

We use direct and indirect speech to communicate words that are spoken by someone. Direct speech conveys the exact words of the speaker by enclosing them within inverted commas. For example:

Larry looked at it and said, 'It is going to be very quiet around here.'

Direct speech is used more often in writing than in speech. Notice the punctuation marks that are used to highlight the words of the speaker.

1. Punctuate the following sentences which are in direct speech.

a. I will make sure that your insurance claim is settled in three months he said.
b. The accountant said open an account to cash your cheque.
c. We told them you have to join our team tomorrow.
d. The doctor said do not smoke.
e. Please take us to visit an industry the students said to their teacher.

Look at the following sentences. The first sentence is in direct speech as it uses the exact words of the narrator. However, when we tell somebody else what the narrator said, we need to use indirect speech. Read the second sentence where the narrator's utterances have been changed into indirect speech.

- When Juan Garzia asked the narrator for his salary, the narrator said, 'Next pay day, Juan. On the Twentieth.'
- When Juan Garcia asked the narrator for his money, the narrator replied that he could get his money on the next pay day, which was the Twentieth.

Some of the changes that happen to a sentence within inverted commas when it is changed into indirect speech are as follows. Note that the form of the verb in the reported sentence changes in the ways listed below only if the reporting verb is in the simple past tense.

The form of the verb within inverted commas changes to the corresponding past tense when the reporting verb is in the simple past tense (e.g., *said*, *told*, *asked*). Look at the following pairs of sentences and note how the verb in the reported sentence changes one tense back in indirect speech.

He said, 'The bell *rings* at 9 a.m.'
He said that the bell *rang* at 9 a.m.
He said, 'The bell *rang*.'
He said that the bell *had rung*.
He said, 'The bell *will ring*.'
He said that the bell *would ring*.
He said, 'Alex *can ring* the bell.'
He said that Alex *could ring* the bell.

Note that the modal auxiliaries 'must' and 'should' either remain unchanged or change to 'had to' or 'would have to'. The modal auxiliary 'ought to' remains unchanged.

He said, 'Alex *must ring* the bell.'
He said that Alex *had to ring* the bell.

In some situations, the simple past tense or the simple present tense form of the verb in direct speech remains unchanged in indirect speech even when the reporting verb is in past tense. Look at the following pairs of sentences.

The speaker said, 'The United Nations *adopted* the Human Rights Charter in 1948.'

The speaker said that the United Nations *adopted* the Human Rights Charter in 1948. (reporting historical events)

They said, 'If it *rained* for three months in the desert, farming *would be* possible there.'
They said that if it *rained* for three months in the desert, farming would *be* possible there. (reporting hypothetical conditionals)

Mira said, 'When the boy *picked up* the baby, his sister *smiled*.'
Mira said that when the boy *picked up* the baby, his sister *smiled*. (reporting two events happening at about the same time)

She said, 'Nitin *takes* the 8 o'clock train every day.'
She said that Nitin *takes* the 8 o'clock train every day. (habitual action/something that is true at the present time)

I said, 'Water *is* essential for life.'
I said that water *is* essential for life. (a universal truth/scientific fact)

Tina said just a minute ago, 'The theatre group *is visiting* our city soon.'
Tina said just a minute ago that the theatre group *is visiting* our city soon. (an event expected to happen in the immediate future)

Another change that occurs when sentences in direct speech are reported in indirect speech is in the form of demonstratives (this, these) and adverbs of time and place (now, ago, today, yesterday, here, etc). Look at the table and a few examples below to understand how this happens. Again note that the words listed below usually change only if the reporting verb is in the simple past tense.

direct speech	**indirect speech**
now	then
here	there
ago	before, earlier
today/tonight	that day/that night
tomorrow	the next day/the following day
yesterday	the previous day/ the day before
last month	the previous month
next week	the following week
this/these	that/those

The man said to me, 'Don't put your things here.'
The man ordered me not to put my things there.
Udit said to his wife, 'When are you going out tomorrow?'
Udit asked his wife when she was going out the next day.
He says to me, 'What is this place called?'
He asks me what this place is called. (not 'that place')

2. Change these sentences into indirect speech.

a. The officer said to the new recruit, 'You have to wear your identity card when you enter the office.'
b. The new recruit said, 'Yes sir, I will wear it right away.'
c. The manager said, 'Please inform me in advance if you are unable to come to work.'
d. The customer asked, 'What is the cost of this product?'
e. Sriram said to his father, 'I am fortunate to have a father like you.'

Memo writing

A memo is a short, internal, written communication from one section of the office to another. That is why it is also called an inter-office memo. In the story, a number of memos are sent from the main office to the junior engineers. Look at the format in which a memo is written.

ABC Gas Company
25, I Avenue
George Bush Road
New Mexico

To: The Junior Engineers
From: The Superintendent
Date: 30.5.2008

Subject: Advance in case of emergency only

There have been too many abuses of the advance-against-wages privilege. Hereafter, no advance against wages will be made to any employee except in a genuine emergency.

Write memos for the following situations.

1. Imagine that you are working as an assistant manager in a company. You are responsible for collecting bills and processing them for payment. You find that you have received more bills than the money you have with you to make the payment. Write a memo to the Finance Officer of your company to allocate more funds to you so that you can process the bills and disburse the money to the people concerned.

2. Assume that you work as a customer care executive in a service company. Your job is to take care of the customers' problems. Your company has given you a landline phone which functions only as an intercom. Customers can call you from outside but you cannot call them directly. You always have to ask the operator to connect you to the customers. Write a memo to the Vice-President, Customer Care, Clinton Service Providers, Navi Mumbai, to provide you with a '0' dialing facility to call customers directly, not only for local calls but also for STD calls.

Thinking about soft skills

Discuss these questions in pairs and answer them briefly.

1. What is adaptability? How is adaptability a survival skill in an organisation?
2. Who needs this skill most in an organisation?
3. How is knowledge of human relations an important dimension of adaptability?
4. How do you maintain your self-respect and yet adjust with others?

Adaptability skills from the story

The narrator and Larry are good at managing both the stokers and the management of the company. They understand the stokers' problem, which is that they need to get an advance on their salary every third or fourth day. While following the company rules, the two engineers make use of the exceptions available, to help the stokers. The main office on the other hand, attempts to stick to the original rule of paying on the fifth and twentieth of every month. It issues one memo after another to discourage the stokers. However, both the junior engineers and the stokers modify their strategies so that they continue to keep their jobs. This is possible due to their innovative thinking and risk taking attitude. The stokers invent many excuses to bend the rules to their advantage, take the risk of resigning their jobs, and assume different names to re-join the company. If they did not adapt themselves, they would suffer and the company would also suffer for want of good stokers.

The tension between the workers and management gets resolved when the junior engineers meet the superintendent to apprise him of the real situation. It is only then that the management takes the trouble to understand the problems of the workers and adapts its administrative rules to suit the needs of the workers without compromising organisational objectives. Thus there is a need for adaptability from both the workers and the management.

Activity

The activities below will help you understand how rapidly changes occur in organisations. If you learn to accept these changes and adapt yourself accordingly, you will not only be an asset to your organisation but also be happy with your work.

1. With the advancements in personal computers and the widespread use of computers and laptops for office purposes, the job of the typist has become a thing of the past. Find out from some middle level and senior level managers how the change has affected their companies. Have typists been forced out of jobs or have they upgraded their skills?
2. Visit a nearby bank or post office and observe the changes that have occurred. Contrast the traditional office with the workplace today. ATM, core banking, multi-city cheque facilities, internet banking, tax collection, phone bill collection, passport application processing, gold coin selling, credit cards, insurance, mutual funds, etc., have flooded banks and post offices. These are not the traditional jobs of the people working in banks and post offices. After you have visited these places write a report on your observations and present it to the class. You may also submit a written report to the class teacher.

Proverbs on adaptability skills

1. Read the following proverbs from various countries about the importance of adaptability. Can you add a few more proverbs from your mother tongue or any other language? Which proverb do you like the most? Why? Share your views with the class.

a. Change yourself and you change the earth.
b. Times change and we with time.
c. A reed before the wind lives on, while mighty oaks do fall.
d. Adversity makes strange bedfellows.
e. The unexpected happens.
f. New lords, new rules.
g. The wise adapt themselves to circumstances as water moulds itself to the pitcher.
h. Circumstances alter cases.
i. The dogs may bark but the caravan moves on.
j. To exist is to change; to change is to mature; to mature is to create oneself endlessly.

2. These proverbs highlight the importance of adaptability. Write a paragraph of 150 words about the need for adapting oneself to different situations in life.

3. **Choose the proverb which best summarises the story and explain your choice to the class.**

Soft skills in the workplace

Work in groups and discuss the following questions.

1. Why do some employees change jobs frequently, while others work loyally for their companies for many years?
2. What are some important areas you will look into before you decide whether a company is suitable for you or not?
3. What are the essential features of good communication in an organisation?

Real life experience

In groups of four or five discuss the advantages and disadvantages of changing jobs frequently. Support your views with examples of people you know who have changed jobs very often. The group leaders may then report their views to the class.

Self-assessment

Read the following 'yes' or 'no' questions carefully. If your answer is YES, write 1. If your answer is NO, write 0.

	Questions	1 or 0
1.	Do you work independently without contant supervision?	
2.	Do you accept the views of others in your team?	
3.	Do you do many tasks at the same time?	
4.	Do you perform well under pressure?	
5.	Do you suggest alternative ways to achieve your organisational goals?	
6.	Do you accept changes readily?	
7.	Do you do work willingly?	
8.	Do you tolerate difficult people around you?	
9.	Do you work without being disturbed by the lack of good facilities?	
10.	Do you take up the work assigned to others in an emergency?	
11.	Do you have the courage to tell the management when there is something seriously wrong?	
12.	Do you follow company rules even if you do not like them?	
13.	Do you adjust to difficult situations?	
14.	Do you set priorities for yourself?	

15. Do you have the ability to solve problems independently?
16. Do you have the knack of switching from one job to another quickly?
17. Do you have an open mind to new ideas and concepts?
18. Do you have a positive attitude?
19. Do you have the ability to take risks?
20. Do you have the persistence to complete jobs?

If your score is between 15–20, you have excellent adaptability skills. If your score is less than 15, you have to improve your adaptability skills.

Further reading

Here are some stories by William E Barrett. Read the stories and if possible, discuss them in the class.

1. The Incredible Ridley
2. With Their Own Weapons
3. The Visitor in Red
4. The Moving Mountain
5. The Living Character
6. Good-bye for Now
7. Successful Contact
8. First Command
9. The Expert
10. Memory Town

9. Non-Verbal Communication Skills

Leading up to the story

Discuss these questions in groups of four or five. The group leader may then present the answers to the class.

1. What is the purpose of education?
2. What do students generally do after completing their undergraduate studies?
3. What does society feel about unemployed youth?
4. What are the various reasons for not having jobs?
5. What role do parents play in helping their children get jobs?
6. What are the various ways of getting jobs?

A real good smile

Read the story by Bill Naughton. Then answer the questions that follow.

At the time I'm talking of, I had reached the age of fourteen, which in those days was school-leaving age. So I shook hands with my teacher, almost dropped a tear on my old wooden desk, said good-bye to all my mates, walked across the playground and through the school gates for the last time, and went home.

Now before I could turn around, you might say, I was in trouble. Yes, I was in disgrace. I couldn't find a job! I was out of work. And I had the feeling that everybody was talking about me behind my back, so that I was ashamed to show my face in the street.

It wasn't really my fault, it was my mother and father's. I know you always try to blame somebody else, but in this case it was true. There were hundreds of jobs going, and I could have had one of them, but you know what parents are; they always think that their own lad is different from every other lad, and they've got to have some special job for him, something with a future in it, as they say. Nine times out of ten it's not the sort of job you want at all.

At that time the spinning-mills were terribly short of 'little piercers.' Now that was the job.

But to go on with the story. My mum and dad wanted me to go and work as an apprentice in the locomotive shed. It was not a good job to start with, but, as they said, it had a great future. If I got the job I would start as a dirt wiper, then in a few years I would become a greaser, and after a long time they would give me an oil can and make me an oiler-and-greaser, then as time went on I would be promoted to a job on the footplate of an engine, and learn to be a fireman and stoke up the engine of the train. Then, with a bit of luck, I might become an engine-driver when I was about fifty. This job might not seem much to boys of today, but in those days anyone who had a job in the loco shed was practically regarded as being royalty, and it needed a lot of influence to get a job there. That was why I was hanging about the house, in disgrace, waiting for this influence to be laid on for me.

Now the man who was going to do it was called Alf Agar. He was our next-door neighbour, and though he was only a common plate layer on the permanent way, he did know an oiler-and-greaser called Tom Petty, and this Tom Petty knew Mr Bidwell, who was the boss of the loco', shed and with a bit of luck he was hoping to persuade Tom to speak for me. But Mr Bidwell was like a headmaster, not the sort of man you could easily approach, so that everything had to be arranged. One Friday evening Alf Agar came in to tell us that it had all been fixed up.

'The first thing I have to tell you,' he said 'is that Mister Bidwell will not give a job to any lad that has been spoken for. He is dead against any kind of influence. He believes that every lad should be able to speak up for himself. So young Billy will have to go there and ask for the job himself.'

'But how do I ask?' I said.

'Come here and I'll show you,' said Alf.

My mum and dad stood by and watched while Alf explained what I had to do to get a job from Mr Bidwell. Alf put his hands on my shoulders. 'Now I'll tell you the first thing Mr Bidwell cannot bear the sight of.'

'What's that?' I said.

'He can't bear the sight of a lad with his hands in his pockets.'

I pulled my hands out of my pockets at once. But my father spotted me. 'I've been telling him for years not to walk about with his hands in his pockets,' he said.

'Now don't shout,' said my mother to my father, 'let us hear what Mr Agar has to say.'

'Mr Bidwell likes to see a lad with his shoulders well back,' went on Alf. At the same time he pushed my shoulders back until my backbone seemed to be splitting. 'An' he likes to see 'em stand as straight an' erect as a Goldstream Guardsman—head back and chin in.'

I straightened up and tried to bring my chin in and stick my chest out. Alf looked at me with a sort of pity, and then he went on with the next instruction.

'Mr Bidwell doesn't allow mumblin' or meemawin', such as, ''D-do y-you w -want any lads, Mister?'' Anything like that drives him mad. You've got to speak up in a loud, clear voice, *''I've come for a job, sir!''* An' be sure and say the *''Sir!''* as though you meant it. Have you got me, Billy?'

It was a lot to keep on my mind; no hands in pockets, a straight back, and chin in, and to speak up in a clear voice, but I nodded to Alf and said that I thought I had got him.

'Now to come to the main point,' said Alf, looking very solemn, 'there is one thing Mister Bidwell must have!'

'What's that?' I said weakly.

'*A real good smile*,' said Alf.

'How do you mean?' I said.

'I mean that he can't bear the sight of a miserable lad. If he saw you looking miserable he would never give you a job, no matter how you were in other respects. He must have a boy with a real good smile.'

Then he turned to my mum and dad and said, 'He's like all bosses; he'd crack his own face if ever he were to attempt to smile. But he can't stand the idea that those who work under him are not happy at their work.' Then Alf turned to me. 'Have you got all that fixed in your mind, Billy?' he asked kindly.

'I think so,' I said.

'What the dickens do you mean by think so!' shouted my father. 'You get it stuck in your mind and keep it there. Or else you have to go and work in the dirty snuffy.'

'I don't care if I do—' I began.

'Hush, hush,' said my mother.

'I think we'd better have a rehearsal,' said Alf.

He turned to me. 'After all, Billy, your whole future depends on that smile. Do you follow me–the job you're doing forty years from to-day will depend on the smile you give to Mr Bidwell.'

'What do you want me to do?' I said.

'*Smile!*' exclaimed my father.

'Steady on,' said Alf, 'let's do it properly.' He looked at me and said, 'Now you go into the back kitchen, Billy.'

'Yes,' I said, 'what then?'

'Imagine you are a lad out of work,' he said.

'That'll be easy,' I said.

'Then come in here,' said Alf, 'and imagine that I am Mr. Bidwell and you've come to ask me for a job. Keep in mind the smile!'

Then I went into the kitchen and I stood there all alone. I didn't feel much like smiling. I stood in front of the looking-glass in the kitchen and tried it out. The awful sight was like a grinning skeleton, and I nearly frightened myself. Perhaps that Bert Hodge at school wasn't entirely wrong when he called me 'a real ugly beggar.' Then I heard Alf call me from the front place.

'Come on, Billy! Let's have a look at you.'

I went in and began to smile. It was hurting my face. My cheeks felt all wrinkled up. I went up to Alf and he looked closely at me. There was a doubtful look in his eyes. 'Can't you show your teeth a bit more?' he said to me.

I showed them a bit more. He didn't seem to care very much for that either. But he was a nice man and he said, 'I'll tell you what to do – keep practicing over the week-end. Do it like this,—' and he began to smile for me and to call out, 'Good morning, sir!'

I had a very busy week-end trying out different smiles. Then came Monday morning, and I set out from home with my shoulders back, my head in the air, and a big smile on my face—until I got round the corner of the street. Then when I knew I was out of sight I put my hands in my pockets, and dropped into my usual slouch, and trudged along a picture of misery.

I thought of all my mates that I had left at school and I envied them their sums and compositions and geography and history. I suddenly realised what a happy life I had left, and what a hard, uncertain world I had moved into. Then I thought of my other mates who had gone to work in the dirty snuffy; they didn't have to hold their shoulders back, or any of that silly nonsense. I had now reached a place called Green Fold, and had to turn into a narrow country road that led to the loco' works. The air was a bit fresher here, and I saw a tree and some grass, and somehow my troubles seemed to lighten for a while. It was quite a long road, and on the right-hand side there was a red-brick building in the middle of some quiet grounds. This was the mental home.

Just ahead of me was a tree stump. And as the road was deserted I decided to have a last rehearsal on my own. I flung back my shoulders, swung my arms, and went marching up to this stump with a big smile on my face.

'Good morning, sir!' I cried out. 'I've come to see about a job. Please don't shake your head, sir, for I will not take no for an answer. I don't want anyone to speak for me, I'll speak for myself—' and I began to take off my jacket and roll up my sleeve. Suddenly I heard a man cough. I turned and saw I was being watched by a gardener from the mental home. His face looked solemn as he spoke to me. 'First on your left,' he said. 'You'll see some big green gates. Once you've got your uniform come across to me because I can use a lad on this job.' I grabbed my jacket and ran off towards the loco' works.

When I got there I felt quite fresh. The shock had worn off, and in some way I felt better than ever. I strode into the shunting yard and I went straight across to what they call the Locomotive Shed. There was a man in overalls holding a great big spanner, who appeared to be taking an engine to pieces. I went up to him and said, 'Please could you tell me where I would find Mr Bidwell?'

'Aye, I could for sure,' he said. 'Can you see that office in the far corner? You go across there and you'll find Mr Bidwell inside. Don't forget to knock on the door. He's a very funny chap.'

'That doesn't worry me. Thanks very much,' I said, and I went walking through the shed. I was a bit of a crafty lad, and it struck me that Mr Bidwell might be peeping through the window, so I walked along with my shoulders back and a smile on my face, and I went straight up to the door and I gave a good firm knock on it.

'Come in,' called a voice.

I turned the door-handle and went in. It was more like a small workshop than an office. There were lots of plans and blue prints around the place, and also some engineer's fine tools hanging from shelves. Mr Bidwell was standing beside his desk. He was a round faced man and not nearly as frightening as I had imagined. I put on a special big smile for him.

'Good morning, sir!' I called out in a loud voice.

'Good morning, laddie,' he said. I could see he was rather pleased at my smiling appearance, as though he wasn't used to people smiling at him.

'I've come for a job, sir,' I said. He was going to say something but I thought it might be better if I said all my piece at once. 'I don't care how I start, sir, I'll soon work my way up. And what's more, I can start this very minute.'

In that moment I could see that I had won him. He was an elderly man, grown old before his time I decided, and he wasn't at all the ogre he had been made out to be. He was smiling warmly at me and I realised the job was mine. I pictured myself on the footplate of the Flying Scotsman on my first long trip, with my mum and dad in the first-class compartment behind. Although he was smiling, there seemed to be a hint of sadness in that smile. I'll cheer him up, I thought, as we work together.

'Now on what job, sir,' I said, 'would you like me to start?'

He hesitated. 'I'm not sure,' he said. 'It's not for me to say, not rightly.'

'Oh, but it is,' I said. 'I'll do anything you tell me.' He shook his head. 'I think it'd be better,' he said, 'if you were to wait and see Mr Bidwell.'

I could hardly believe my ears. 'M-mister who?'

'Mr Bidwell,' he said. 'I'm only the sweeper-up.'

My heart seemed to sink right down into my stomach. I felt my shoulders sag back to their old position. My hands went into my trouser pockets. To think that wonderful performance had all been wasted! He was only a sweeper-up. All my energy had gone. He turned to me quickly as footsteps were heard outside. Through the glass door I saw a tall man with a hard snooty face. The sweeper-up whispered, 'Here's Mr Bidwell now!'

The door burst open and in he came. He had an enormous square jaw and narrow eyes and big, black, bushy eyebrows. He looked at me and let out what sounded like a bark. 'Who do you want?'

'D-do-y-you w-want any lads, mister?' I mumbled.

He glared at me. 'Eh? What? Speak up!' he roared. 'I can't hear a word you say.'

I didn't take my hands out of my pockets, I didn't straighten up. I just said: 'Do you want any lads?'

'Lads! lads!' he ranted at me. 'No! I don't want any lads. Certainly not a specimen like you! I wouldn't take you on at any cost!'

Suddenly I felt a bit of courage or something of the sort rise up in me. 'No,' I said, 'an' I wouldn't jolly well take *you* on at any cost!'

I could see that shook him. I expect he had never been spoken to like that in his life. I walked to the door with my hands in my pockets, and as I was going out I said to the sweeper-up, 'S'long, mate. I wouldn't have your job at any price.'

I felt better for having spoken my mind. I went straight to Taylor and Brown's Spinning Mill and I asked for my pal, Jimmy Ackers, who was a little piercer there. I started in the spinning-mill that very day.

When I got home that evening, Alf Agar came into our house. 'Billy,' he said, 'Mr Bidwell wants you to start at the loco' shed tomorrow morning.'

'Have you gone crazy?' I said.

'It's a fact,' he said. 'He liked the way you spoke up to him. He felt you were an honest lad. If there's one thing that he admires it's honesty.'

So that's how it was; one day I was out of work and the next day I had two jobs. I was sorry to leave the snuffy, because I had some nice mates there. But I had to admit prospects were better in the loco' shed. Of course I never spoke like that to Mr Bidwell again.

He liked you to speak your mind, but once was enough. It was a good way to get a job, but it would be a good way to lose one if you overdid it.

Bill Naughton

Understanding the story

Answer the following questions. Later you may discuss your answers in the class.

1. Why is the boy in trouble?
2. What are the five stages of career growth in the locomotive shed?
3. Why is it difficult to get a job at the locomotive shed?
4. What tips does Alf Agar give Billy?
5. Why does Agar emphasise that Billy should give a real good smile?
6. What happens to Billy near the mental home?
7. How does Billy perform in front of the sweeper-up?
8. How does Billy behave in front of Mr Bidwell?
9. Why does Billy join Jimmy Ackers at the spinning mill?
10. What news does Alf Agar bring at the end?
11. What are the two career choices open to Billy and which one does he choose?
12. What qualities of a job seeker are emphasised in the story?

Understanding people

The main characters in the story have certain traits that define them. Write down the characteristics of each person in the story and complete the table.

Characters	Characteristics
1. Billy	
2. Billy's dad	
3. Billy's mum	
4. Alf Agar	
5. Mr Bidwell	

Vocabulary development

Meanings in context

Look up a dictionary and find the meanings of the words and phrases below, as they are used in the context of the story.

Words and phrases	Meanings
1. disgrace	
2. piercers	
3. royalty	
4. bear the sight of	
5. mumbling	
6. meemawing	
7. respects	
8. what the dickens	
9. snuffy	
10. slouch	
11. trudge	
12. deserted	
13. crafty	
14. ogre	
15. made out	
16. snooty	
17. ranted	
18. prospects	

`Wh' and 'Yes' or 'No' questions

In any interaction with others we ask and answer questions. There are two types of questions: 'Wh' questions and 'Yes' or 'No' questions. 'Wh' questions are considered to be open-ended questions for which we have to give detailed answers, with some information and explanation. 'Yes' or 'No' questions require us to say 'yes' or 'no' and nothing more. Hence these questions are called close-ended questions. They do not encourage much interaction, whereas 'wh' questions allow for extended interaction.

'Wh' questions

These questions begin with 'wh' words (except *how*): *what, when, where, why, who and how.*

Read the following examples.

- What is a positive attitude?
- When did you resign from your last job?
- Where did you have your school education?
- How did you come to know about our company?
- Why do you want this job?

'Yes' or 'No' questions

These questions are framed by using the helping verbs *be*, *have* and, *do*, and their various forms: *is*, *was*, *am*, *are*, *were*, *has*, *had*, *have*, *does*, *did*, *do*, etc.

Read the following examples.

- Is your name Mr Girish Ramachandran?
- Was your experience as an intern a useful one?
- Am I right?
- Are you from Tuticorin?
- Were you aware of our company in your school days?
- Has anybody helped you acquire a new skill?
- Have you worked in a team before?
- Does your college offer a campus placement service?
- Do you enjoy working with people?

Enact the different situations below. Practice using 'wh' and 'yes' or 'no' type of questions when you do the role play.

1. You have completed your undergraduate studies. You have not got a job, nor have you joined an institution for higher studies. You happen to meet your father's close friend Mr Ajay Karthick. He is interested in your future plans and asks you a series of questions, which you answer. Work with a partner and write down the questions and answers before you do the role play.
2. You work for a well-known automobile company. You happen to meet your college mate Mr Rajesh Khanna who works in the marketing division of an automobile company in California, USA. Have a conversation with your friend to find out whether you could have tie-ups to sell some of your products in the US market. Work with a partner and write down the dialogue before you role play the conversation.

Working on articulation and gestures

Here is a list of utterances from the story. Say each sentence using different tones of voice and gestures. You should be able to communicate different meanings when you change your tone and gestures.

1. 'But how do I ask?'
2. 'What's that?'
3. 'He can't bear the sight of a lad with his hands in his pockets.'
4. 'How do you mean?'
5. 'I think we'd better have a rehearsal.'
6. 'Come on, Billy! Let's have a look at you.'

Thinking about soft skills

Work in pairs and discuss these questions.

1. When you speak to someone, how do you know that they are interested in what you are saying?
2. When you visit someone, how do you know if they are welcoming you?
3. When do you say, 'I beg your pardon,' 'please repeat,' 'I can't hear you,' etc., in your conversation with others?
4. What role does a smile play in human communication?
5. How do you understand whether somebody needs help or not?

Non-verbal communication skills from the story

Language is a tool for communication. But it plays only a small role in human communication. According to Albert Mehrabian who has studied non-verbal communication, the spoken word conveys only 7 percent of the message. A larger part of any message is communicated through vocal and visual elements. Vocal elements include the quality, speed, loudness, pitch and intonation of the voice. Mehrabian attributes 38 percent of communication to these vocal elements. But 55 percent of communication takes place through visual elements which include gestures, postures, distance, smell and touch. So, it is necessary to cultivate effective non-verbal communication skills.

Activity

1. **Read the instructions Alf Agar gives to Billy. List them under the three behavioural headings in the table below. Two have been done for you.**

	Visual	Vocal	Verbal
1.	Hands in pockets		Good morning, Sir!
2.			
3.			
4.			
5.			
6.			

2. **Work with a partner and make a list of things you can do to improve your non-verbal communication skills.**

Proverbs on non-verbal communication skills

1. **Read the following proverbs on non-verbal communication skills from various countries. Can you add a few more proverbs from your mother tongue or any other language? Which proverb do you like the most? Why? Share your views with the class.**

    a. Actions speak louder than words.
    b. The face is the index of the mind.
    c. Speech is silver and silence is golden.

d. A picture is worth a thousand words.
e. Example is better than precept.
f. The eyes are the windows to the soul.
g. Argument is the worst kind of communication.
h. Words may show a man's wit, but actions his meaning.
i. Attitudes are the real figures of speech.

2. **These proverbs emphasise the fact that words alone are not enough to communicate effectively. Sometimes our words may convey one meaning whereas our actions will convey quite another.**

   Write a paragraph of 150 words on the necessity of matching our words with our deeds in order to communicate effectively.

Soft skills at the workplace

Work in groups and discuss the following situations focusing on the non-verbal messages that are being communicated.

1. A company announces a bonus for its employees but it does not disburse the bonus even a month after the announcement.
2. The management and the workers of a company sign a memorandum of understanding to share the profits after taxes and paying dividends to shareholders. However, the management deliberately runs the company into losses.
3. Your teacher tells you that he will take special classes for you on Saturdays. Most students turn up for the special class. But the teacher does not appear.
4. You ask your father to buy you a new cell phone. He promises to buy the cell phone on the first of the next month. You remind him a number of times but each time he postpones it to a later date.
5. A member of your staff comes in late every day. Specify the non-verbal, verbal and official methods you would use to deal with him.

Real life experience

Wherever you go, make a conscious effort to observe the body language of people. You will learn a great deal about human nature. You can also observe your friends and share your observations about their behaviour with them.

Self-assessment

Read the following yes or no questions carefully. If your answer is YES, write 1. If your answer is NO, write 0.

	Questions	1 or 0
1.	Do you maintain eye contact when speaking or listening to someone?	
2.	Do you smile frequently?	
3.	Do you have a firm handshake?	
4.	Do you have an awareness of how you use space while communicating with others?	
5.	Do you sit up and stand straight when you interact with others?	
6.	Do you take care of your hygiene?	
7.	Do you dress appropriately?	
8.	Do you speak loudly and clearly?	
9.	Do you use gestures that match your message?	
10.	Do you nod your head appropriately to indicate yes or no?	
11.	Do you use humour to relieve tension?	
12.	Do you lean forward towards the person you are interacting with?	
13.	Do you move your legs and hands unnecessarily?	
14.	Do you vary the pitch and tone of your voice to avoid monotony?	
15.	Do you pause at suitable moments for your listeners to grasp your ideas?	
16.	Do you use gestures that encourage others?	
17.	Do you hold your body in a relaxed manner?	
18.	Do you breathe normally?	
19.	Do you shift the focus of your eyes from time to time?	
20.	Do you complete your sentences?	

If your score is between 15–20, you have excellent non-verbal communication skills. If your score is less than 15, you have to improve your non-verbal communication skills.

Further reading

Bill Naughton has written a collection of wonderful stories which you can read in his book *The Goal Keeper's Revenge and Other Stories*. Later on you may discuss them in class.

10. Written Communication Skills

Leading up to the story

Discuss these questions in groups of four or five. The group leader may then present the answers to the class.

1. When and why do people retire from employment?
2. How do retired people generally spend their life?
3. What are some creative activities that retired people can pursue?
4. Do you know of any retired employees who continue to get appreciation from their old employers? In what form do the employers show their appreciation?

Gateman's gift

Read the story by R K Narayan. Then answer the questions that follow.

When a dozen persons question openly or slyly a man's sanity, he begins to entertain serious doubts about himself. This is what happened to ex-gateman Govind Singh. And you could not blame the public either. What could you do with a man who carried about in his hand a registered postal cover and asked, 'Please tell me what there is inside?' The obvious answer was, 'Open it and see ....' He seemed horrified at this suggestion. 'Oh no, no, can't do it,' he declared and moved off to another friend and acquaintance. Everywhere the suggestion was the same till he thought everyone had turned mad. And then somebody said, 'If you don't like to open it and yet want to know what is inside you must take it to the X-ray Institute.' This was suggested by an ex-compounder who lived in the next street.

'What is it?' asked Govind Singh. It was explained to him. 'Where is it?' He was directed to the City X-ray Institute.

But before saying anything further about his progress, it would be useful to go back to an earlier chapter in his history. After war service in 1914–1918, he came to be recommended for a gatekeeper's post at Engladia's. He liked the job very much. He was given a khaki uniform, a resplendent band across his shoulder and a short stick. He gripped the stick and sat down on a stool at the entrance of the office. And when his chief's car pulled up at the gate he stood at attention and gave a military salute. The office consisted of a staff numbering over a hundred and as they trooped in and out every day he kept an eye on them. At the end of the day he awaited the footsteps of the General Manager coming down the stairs and rose stiffly and stood at attention, and after he left, the hundreds of staff poured out. The doors were shut; Singh carried his stool in, placed it under the staircase, and placed his stick across it. Then he came out and the main door was locked and sealed. In this way he had spent twenty-five years of service, and then he begged to be pensioned off. He would not have thought of retirement yet, but for the fact that he found his sight and hearing playing tricks on him; he could not catch the Manager's footsteps on the stairs, and it was hard to recognise him even at ten yards. He was ushered into the presence of the chief, who looked up for a moment from his papers and muttered: 'We are very pleased with your work for us, and the company will give you a pension of twelve rupees for your life ....' Singh clicked his heels, saluted, turned on his heel and went out of the room with his heart brimming with gratitude and pride. This was the second occasion when the great man had spoken to him, the first being on the first day of his service. As he had stood at his post, the chief, entering the office just then, looked up for a moment and asked, 'Who are you?'

'I'm the new gatekeeper, master,' he had answered. And he spoke again only on this day. Though so little was said, Singh felt electrified on both occasions by the words of his master. In Singh's eyes the chief had acquired a sort of godhood, and it would be quite adequate if a god spoke to one only once or twice in a lifetime. In moments of contemplation Singh's mind dwelt on the words of his master, and on his personality.

His life moved on smoothly. The pension together with what his wife earned by washing and sweeping in a couple of houses was quite sufficient for him. He ate his food, went out and met a few friends, slept and spent some evenings sitting at a cigarette shop which his cousin owned. This tenor of life was disturbed on the first of every month when he donned his old khaki suit, walked to his old office, and salammed the accountant at the counter and received his pension. Sometimes if it was closing he waited on the roadside for the General Manager to come down, and saluted him as he got into his car.

There was a lot of time around him, an immense sea of leisure. In this state he made a new discovery about himself, that he could make fascinating models out of clay and wood dust. The discovery came suddenly, when one day a child in the neighbourhood brought to him its little doll for repair. He not only repaired it but made a new thing of it. This discovery pleased him so much that he very soon became absorbed in it. His backyard gave him a plentiful supply of pliant clay, and the carpenter's shop next to his cousin's cigarette shop sawdust. He purchased paint for a few annas. And lo! He found his hours gliding. He sat there in the front part of his home, bent over his clay, and brought into existence a miniature universe; all the colours of life were there, all the forms and creatures, but of the size of his middle finger; whole villages and towns were there, all the persons he had seen passing before his office when he was sentry there—that beggar woman coming at midday, and that cucumber vendor; he had the eye of a cartoonist for human faces. Everything went down into clay. It was a wonderful miniature reflection of the world; and he mounted them neatly on thin wooden slices, which enhanced their attractiveness. He kept these in his cousin's shop and they attracted huge crowds every day and sold very briskly. More than the sales Singh felt an ecstasy when he saw admiring crowds clustering round his handiwork.

On his next pension day he carried to his office a street scene (which he ranked as his best), and handed it over the counter to the accountant with the request: 'Give this to the Sahib, please!'

'All right,' said the accountant with a smile. It created a sensation in the office and disturbed the routine of office working for nearly half an hour. On the next pension day he carried another model (children at play) and handed it over the counter.

'Did Sahib like the last one?'

'Yes, he liked it.'

'Please give this one to him—' and he passed it over the counter. He made it a convention to carry on every pension day an offering for his master, and each time his greatest reward was the accountant's stock reply to his question: 'What did the Sahib say?'

'He said it was very good.'

At last he made his masterpiece. A model of his office frontage with himself at his post, a car at the entrance, and the chief getting down; this composite model was so realistic that while he sat looking at it, he seemed to be carried back to his office days. He passed it over the counter on his pension day and it created a very great sensation in the office. 'Fellow, you have not left yourself out either!' people cried and looked admiringly at Singh. A sudden fear seized Singh and he asked: 'The master won't be angry, I hope?'

'No, no, why should he be?' said the accountant, and Singh received his pension and went home.

A week later when he was sitting on the *pyol* kneading clay, the postman came and said: 'A registered letter for you....'

'For me!' Any letter would have upset Singh; he had received less than three letters in his lifetime, and each time it was torture for him till the contents were read out. Now a registered letter! 'Only lawyers send registered letters, isn't it so?'

'Usually,' said the postman.

'Please take it back. I don't want it,' said Singh.

'Shall I say "Refused"?' asked the postman, 'No, no,' said Singh. 'Just take it back and say you have not found me ....'

'That I can't do ....' said the postman looking serious. Singh seemed to have no option but to scrawl his signature and receive the packet. He sat gloomily—gazing at the floor. His wife who had gone out and just returned saw him in this condition and asked: 'What is it?' His voice choked as he replied, 'It has come.' He flung at her the registered letter. 'What is it?' she asked. He said, 'How should I know. Perhaps our ruin ....' He broke down. His wife watched him for a moment, went in to attend to some domestic duty and returned, still found him in the same condition, and asked, 'Why not open it and see, ask someone to read it?' He threw up his arms in horror, 'Woman, you don't know what you are saying. It cannot be opened. They have perhaps written that my pension is stopped, and God knows what else the Sahib has said ....'

'Why not go to office and find out from them?'

'Not I! I will never show my face there again ....' replied Singh. 'I have lived without a single remark being made against me, all my life. Now!' He shuddered at the thought of it. 'I knew I was getting into trouble when I made that office model ....' After deeper reflection he said, 'Every time I took something there, people crowded round, stopped all work for nearly an hour .... That must also have reached the Sahib's ears.'

He wandered about saying the same, with the letter in his pocket. He lost taste for food, wandered about unkempt, with his hair standing up like a halo—an unaccustomed sight, his years in military service having given him habitual tidiness. His wife lost all peace of mind and became miserable about him. He stood at the crossroads, clutching the letter in his hand. He kept asking everyone he came across: 'Tell me, what is there in this?' but he would not brook the suggestion to open it and see its contents.

So forthwith Singh found his way to the City X-ray Institute at Race Course Road. As he entered the gate, he observed dozens of cars parked along the drive, and a Gurkha watchman at the gate. Some people were sitting on sofas reading books and journals. They turned and threw a brief look at him and resumed their studies. As Singh stood uncertainly at the doorway, an assistant came up and asked, 'What do you want?' Singh gave a salute, held up the letter uncertainly and muttered, 'Can I know what is inside this?' The assistant made the obvious suggestion. But Singh replied, 'They said you could tell me what's inside without opening it—.' The assistant asked, 'Where do you come from?' Singh explained his life, work and outlook and concluded, 'I've lived without remark all my life. I knew trouble was coming—' There were tears on his cheeks. The assistant looked at him curiously as scores of others had done before, smiled, and said, 'Go home and rest. You are not all right .... Go, go home.'

'Can't you say what is in this?' Singh asked pathetically. The assistant took it in his hand, examined it and said, 'Shall I open it?' 'No, no, no,' Singh cried and snatched it back. There was a look of terror in his eyes. The assembly looked up from their pages and watched him with mild amusement in their eyes. The assistant kindly put his arms on his shoulder and led him out. 'You get well first, and then come back. I tell you —you are not all right.'

Walking back home, he pondered over it. 'Why are they all behaving like this, as if I were a mad man?' When this word came to his mind, he stopped abruptly in the middle of the road, and cried, 'Oh! That's it, is that it? — Mad! Mad!' He shook his head gleefully as if the full truth had just dawned upon him. He now understood the looks the people threw at him. 'Oh! Oh!' he cried aloud. He laughed. He felt a curious relief at this realisation. 'I have been mad and didn't know ....' He cast his mind back. Every little action of his for the last so many days seemed mad; particularly the doll-making. 'What sane man would make clay dolls after twenty-five years of respectable service in an office?' He felt a tremendous freedom of limbs, and didn't feel it possible to walk at an ordinary pace. He wanted to fly. He swung his arms up and down and ran on with a whoop. He ran through the Market Road. When people stood about and watched, he cried, 'Hey, don't laugh at a mad man, for who knows, you will also be mad when you come to make clay dolls,' and charged into their midst with a war cry. When he saw children coming out of a school, he felt it would be nice to amuse their young hearts by behaving like a tiger. So he fell on his hands and knees and crawled up to them with a growl.

He went home in a terrifying condition. His wife who was grinding chilli in the backyard looked up and asked, 'What is this?' His hair hair was covered with street dust; his body was splashed with mud. He could not answer because he choked with mirth as he said: 'Fancy what has happened?'

'What is it?'

'I'm mad, mad.' He looked at his work-basket in a corner, scooped out the clay and made a helmet of it and put it on his head. Ranged on the floor was his latest handiwork. After his last visit to the office he had been engaged in making a model village. It was a resplendent group; a dun road, red tiles, green coconut trees swaying, and the colour of the sarees of the village women carrying water pots. He derived the inspiration for it from a memory of his own village days. It was the most enjoyable piece of work that he had so far undertaken. He lived in a kind of ecstasy while doing it. 'I am going to keep this for myself. A memento of my father's village,' he declared. 'I will show it at an exhibition, where they will give me a medal.' He guarded it like a treasure: when it was wet, he never allowed his wife to walk within ten yards of it: 'Keep off, we don't want your foot dust for this village ....'

Now in his madness, he looked down on it. He raised his foot and stamped everything down into a multi-coloured jam. They were still half-wet. He saw a donkey grazing in the street. He gathered up the jam and flung it at the donkey with the remark, 'Eat this if you like. It is a nice village ....' And he went out on a second round. This was a quieter outing. He strode on at an even pace, breathing deeply, with the clay helmet on, out of which peeped his grey hair, his arms locked behind, his fingers clutching the fateful letter, his face tilted towards the sky. He walked down the Market Road, with a feeling that he was the sole occupant of this globe: his madness had given him a sense of limitless freedom, strength and buoyancy. The remarks and jeers of the crowds gaping at him did not in the least touch him.

While he walked thus, his eye fell on the bulb of a tall street lamp. 'Bulb of the size of a papaya fruit!' he muttered and chuckled. It had been a long cherished desire in him to fling a stone at it; now he felt, in his joyous and free condition, that he was free from the trammels of convention and need not push back any inclination. He picked up a pebble and threw it with good aim. The shattering noise of glass was as music to his ears. A policeman put his hand on his shoulder: 'Why did you do it?' Singh looked indignant. 'I like to crack the glass papaya fruit, that is all,' was the reply. The constable said: 'Come to the station.'

'Oh, yes, when I was in Mesopotamia they put me on half-ration once,' he said, and walked on to the station. He paused, tilted his head to the side and remarked, 'This road is not straight ....' A few carriages and cycles were coming up to him. He found that everything was wrong about them. They seemed to need some advice in the matter. He stopped in the middle of the road, stretched out his arms and shouted, 'Halt!' The carriages stopped, the cyclists jumped off and Singh began a lecture, 'When I was in Mesopotamia—I will tell you fellows who don't know anything about anything.' The policeman dragged him away to the side, and waved to the traffic to resume. One of the cyclists who resumed jumped off the saddle again and came towards him with, 'Why! It is Singh! Singh, what fancy dress is this? What is the matter?' Even through the haze of his insane vision Singh could recognise the voice and the person—the accountant at the office. Singh clicked his heels and gave a salute. 'Excuse me, sir, didn't intend to stop you. You may pass ....' He pointed the way generously, and the accountant saw the letter in his hand. He recognised it although it was mud-stained and crumpled.

'Singh, you got our letter?'

'Yes, sir,—Pass. Do not speak of it ....'

'What is the matter?' He snatched it from his hand. 'Why haven't you opened it?' He tore open the envelope and took out a letter and read aloud: 'The General Manager greatly appreciates the very artistic models you have sent, and he is pleased to sanction a reward of Rs.100 and hopes it will be an encouragement for you to keep up this interesting hobby.'

It was translated to him word for word, and the enclosure, a cheque for one hundred rupees, was handed to him. A big crowd gathered to watch this scene. Singh pressed the letter to his eyes. He beat his brow, and wailed, 'Tell me, sir, am I mad or not?'

'You look quite well, you aren't mad,' said the accountant. Singh fell at his feet and said with tears choking his voice, 'You are a God, sir, to say that I am not mad, I am so happy to hear it.'

On the next pension day he turned up spruce as ever at the office counter. As they handed him the envelope they asked, 'What toys are you making now?'

'Nothing sir. Never again. It is no occupation for a sane man ....' he said, received his pension, and stiffly walked out of the office.

R K Narayan

Understanding the story

Answer the following questions. Later you may discuss your answers in the class.

1. Who is Govind Singh and what problem does he face?
2. Why does he go to the X-ray institute?
3. Why do you think Narayan narrates the earlier part of Govind Singh's life?
4. Why does Govind Singh choose to retire from service?
5. How does the company reward him on his retirement?
6. How many times has the master spoken to Govind Singh?
7. What did Govind Singh find out about himself after retirement?
8. Why is he disturbed when he receives a registered letter from the company?
9. What kind of mad things does Govind Singh do after he receives the letter?
10. Who cures him of his madness?
11. What are the contents of the letter?
12. What does Govind Singh decide to do in the end?

Understanding people

Give brief descriptions of how Govind Singh and each of the characters in the story communicate with each other, and complete the table. For example, are they hostile, friendly, indifferent, encouraging or concerned?

Govind Singh and …	Description of their communication
1. … the General Manager	
2. … the accountant	
3. … the wife	
4. … assistant at the X-ray institute	
5. … the people of the village	

Vocabulary development

Meanings in context

Look up a dictionary and find the meanings of the words and phrases below, as they are used in the context of the story.

Words and phrases	Meanings
1. sanity	
2. resplendent	

3. contemplation
4. immense
5. pliant
6. ecstasy
7. convention
8. scrawl
9. halo
10. abruptly
11. dawned upon
12. whoop
13. buoyancy
14. trammel
15. inclination
16. spruce

Punctuation

Punctuation plays a significant role in effective written communication. The most commonly used punctuation marks are the following:

full stops, commas, colons, question marks, exclamation marks, quotation marks, round brackets, hyphens, dashes, apostrophes

Look at the chart below to understand how these punctuation marks are used.

	Punction mark	When to use it
1.	Full stop [.]	At the end of a sentence; in abbreviations
2.	Question mark [?]	At the end of sentence that asks a question
3.	Exclamation mark [!]	At the end of a sentence to indicate emotions like surprise, alarm, anger, etc.
4.	Quotation marks [‘ ’]	To indicate the exact words spoken by a person
5.	Apostrophe [’]	To indicate possession or ownership; in contractions to indicate where letters have been left out
6.	Hyphen [-]	To attach a prefix to a root; to form compound words
7.	Round brackets or parenthesis [( )]	To include words that offer further clarification to the meaning of a sentence but are not essential to understanding the meaning of the sentence itself

8.	Colon [:]	To introduce a list of items; to give an explanation or additional information
9.	Dash [–]	To add information or explain something; double dashes can be used like brackets.
10.	Comma [,]	To indicate a pause in a sentence or to separate items in a list
11.	Semicolon [;]	To link two closely related sentences

Read the following passages which have been reproduced without any punctuation. Then punctuate the passage and read them again. Do you see how correct punctuation contributes to meaning?

(Both passages have been taken from stories written by Oscar Wilde—the first from 'The Selfish Giant', and the second, from the 'Model Millionaire'.)

1. every afternoon as they were coming from school the children used to play in the giants garden it was a lovely garden with soft green grass here and there over the grass stood beautiful flowers like stars and there were twelve peach trees that in the spring time broke out into delicate blossoms of pink and pearl and in autumn bore rich fruit the birds sat on the trees and sang so sweetly that the children used to stop their games in order to listen to them how happy we were here they cried to each other.
2. unless one is wealthy there is no use in being a charming fellow romance is the privilege of the rich not the profession of the unemployed the poor should be practical and prosaic it is better to have a permanent income than to be fascinating these are the great truths of modern life which hughie erskine never realized poor hughie intellectually we must admit he was not of much importance he never said a brilliant or even an illnatured thing in his life but then he was wonderfully good looking with his crisp brown hair his clearcut profile and his grey eyes he was as popular with men as he was with women and he had every accomplishment except that of making money

Common errors

Many of us for whom English is not a mother tongue tend to make some typical errors in our usage. Here are some areas where we commonly make mistakes when we write and speak.

- Articles — * Egg is boiling on stove.
- Subject-verb agreement — * Everyone are going to the match.
- Tenses — * He will talk regularly on the phone.

* I am having a red Maruti car.
- Pronouns — * This is she's.
- Connectives — * It was pouring. Furthermore, the match was cancelled.
- Vocabulary * — He runs fastly.
- Parts of speech - * Could you advice me, please?
- Number — * The equipments have been cleaned.
- Inversion in questions — * You are coming to my house?

Correct the following sentences.

1. Sun rises in east.
2. Sehwag is one of the best captain of Indian cricket.
3. She has gone to Delhi yesterday.
4. Sita saw he's friend at a restaurant.
5. This is a good company and it does not give casual leave to its employees.
6. Your carrier objective is a worthwhile one.
7. My guest arrived lately.
8. I am having a Honda City car.
9. Foreign tourists generally enjoy the beautiful sceneries in Kunnur.
10. What I can do for you?
11. Ranjit is a sincere worker. He works hardly.
12. We are understanding the problem now.
13. I have studied in one of the best college in India.
14. My supervisor has visited my branch office on 7 June 2008.
15. Please ask him what will he do.
16. One of the boys have qualified in the entrance test.
17. No sooner he had finished college than he found a job.
18. Anu plays violin.
19. Many women are having iron deficiency due to poor nutrition.
20. The painting is too beautiful

Thinking about soft skills

Work in pairs and discuss these questions.

1. What are the many forms of written communication in an organisation?
2. What is an official letter?
3. What is a covering letter?
4. What is an enclosure?
5. What are the various occasions for writing official letters?

Written Communication skills from the story

The 'Gateman's Gift' points to a serious problem in our administrative set up. What to write, when to write, whom to write to, how to write, and why we write are questions which are not commonly addressed in many organisations. As with any other type of communication, written communication too requires that we be sensitive to the person we are writing to.

In this story, the problem was not with the contents of the message but in the way the message was delivered—through a registered letter. The management of the company did not foresee that a registered letter would drive a normal, healthy man like Gobind Singh to the point of madness. We need to think carefully before we send written messages to anyone.

Activity

1. Talk to people you know and find out how many of them fear receiving official letters. Make a list of reasons for their fear and share it with the class.
2. Collect documents regarding the buying and selling of land and discuss the style of writing and its readability.
3. The internet is a good place to look for samples of interesting and useful writing. Choose a piece of writing you particularly like and share it with your group members. Discuss the elements that make it interesting.
4. An important part of written communication is coherence. This means that the various ideas in a piece of writing should fit together logically and sequentially. The sentences in the paragraph below are in a jumbled order. Rewrite them in the correct order to make a sensible paragraph.

   He earned a Masters in Mathematics from the University of Andhra Pradesh in 2005. He worked for a while in a software company in India as an executive. He did his schooling from St John's Higher Secondary School in Hyderabad. Currently, he is a systems manager with a leading IT solutions company in the USA. He obtained his B.Sc. in Mathematics from the Narayanaguda College, affiliated to the University of Andhra Pradesh, in 2003. He gained recognition for his ability to apply mathematical principles to data security from the Ramanujan Institute of Mathematical Sciences. He worked on some major mathematical puzzles that intrigue academicians. Mr Krishna Kumar was born on 21 September 1980.

Proverbs on written communication skills

1. Read the following proverbs on written communication skills from various countries. Can you add a few more proverbs from your mother tongue or any other language? Which proverb do you like the most? Why? Share your views with the class.

a. Words fly, writing remains.
b. The word that is heard perishes, but the letter that is written remains.
c. The palest ink is better than the sharpest memory.
d. Learn to handle a writing-brush and you will never handle a begging bowl.
e. Even the best writer has to erase.
f. Write what you know.
g. Teach the writer, not the writing.
h. Never write a letter when you are angry.
i. Writing makes a perfect man.
j. Writing is 10 percent inspiration and 90 percent perspiration.

2. Some of these proverbs tell you about the value and importance of writing. Others point to the hard work required to achieve effective writing skills and still others point to the need to think clearly before we write.

Write a paragraph of 150 words on how writing is a form of discipline which can help us to improve ourselves.

Soft skills in the workplace

1. Work in groups and discuss the following questions.

a. Why is it important to choose the correct channel of communication?
b. Why do you think many official messages fail to communicate the intended meanings to the recipients?
c. What do we need to keep in mind when we communicate through writing?

2. Work in pairs and discuss the advantages and disadvantages of official written communications. Then fill in the following table.

Features	Advantages	Disadvantages
Speed		
Verifiability		
Distance		
Cost		
Ease of understanding		
Planning		

Real life experience

Interview someone you know who has retired from work. Use the following points to ask the person questions about the job they did. Then write a paragraph on the person's experiences at work. Later, you may share your writing in class.

1. Name of company
2. Nature of the job
3. Date of joining
4. Various positions held
5. Contribution to the company
6. Recognition and reward from the company
7. Reasons for retirement
8. Contact with the company after retirement
9. Unforgettable experiences of meeting with high level officials of the company
10. Company's benefits for the employees
11. Reasons for recommending the company to others

Self-assessment

Read the following 'yes' or 'no' questions carefully. If your answer is YES, write 1. If your answer is NO, write 0.

	Questions	1 or 0
1.	Do you identify the best medium of communication to convey a particular message?	
2.	Do you support your chosen medium with other ways of communication?	
3.	Do you get feedback in response to all communications?	
4.	Do you fill in any gaps in your communication?	
5.	Do you take corrective measures in your communication system?	
6.	Do you give clear instructions to others to do something for you?	
7.	Do you step in to help or guide your staff and colleagues to achieve their goals?	
8.	Do you understand the communication needs of colleagues?	
9.	Do you recognise other's talents and appreciate them in a way in which they can understand you?	
10.	Do you stop to think whether your written communication is absolutely necessary?	
11.	Do you understand the role of writing in your work environment?	

12. Do you write in a variety of formats – letter, memo, report, proposal, etc.?
13. Do you examine and evaluate your own writing?
14. Do you know where to get help with your writing?
15. Do you understand the importance of your target audience?
16. Do you know different ways of documentation and referencing?
17. Do you check your grammar, spelling, and layout?
18. Do you support your writing with suitable tables, charts, or graphs?
19. Do you help others to improve their writing?
20. Do you make the effort to read good writing?
21. Do you revise and edit your own writing often?

If your score is between 15–21, you have good written communication skills. If your score is less than 15, you have to improve your written communication skills.

Further Reading

R K Narayan is a well-known writer with numerous collections of short stories and novels.

Here are some titles you can read. Later on you may discuss them in class.

1. An Astrologer's Day
2. Under the Banyan Tree
3. The Doctor's Word
4. Lawley Road
5. A Horse and Two Goats